C000061666

# Whisky

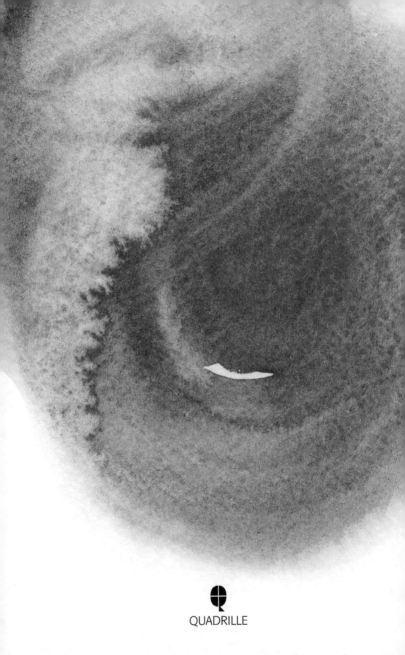

# The knowledge.
**Whisky** | Dave Waddell

For Tash and Otto, with love.

**Publishing consultant** Jane O'Shea
**Editor** Simon Davis
**Creative director** Helen Lewis
**Art direction & design** Claire Peters
**Illustrator** Claire Peters
**Production** Vincent Smith, Tom Moore

First published in 2015 by
Quadrille Publishing Limited
www.quadrille.co.uk

Quadrille is an imprint of Hardie Grant.
www.hardiegrant.com.au

Text © 2015 Dave Waddell
Design and layout © 2015
Quadrille Publishing Limited

Cataloguing in Publication Data:
a catalogue record for this book
is available from the British Library.

ISBN 978 184949 625 4

Printed in the UK

INTRODUCTION 6

1 IN THE NAME OF WHISKY  8
2 FROM GRAIN TO GLASS  20
3 THE ART OF THE DISTILLER  30
4 MASTER OF THE BLEND  44
5 SCOTLAND: THE LABYRINTH
   OF UISGE BEATHA  56
6 AMERICA: BOURBON REBORN  68
7 JAPAN: THE POST-PERFECT OF COPY  78
8 IRELAND: A NEW MOON  88
9 CANADA: BIG IS BEAUTIFUL  100
10 CRAFT AND OTHER WHISKY:
   A BRAVE NEW WORLD  110
11 BEAUTY BEFORE AGE AND OTHER SURPRISES  118
12 A STORM IN A WHISKY GLASS  130
13 A ROUGH GUIDE TO DRINKING WHISKY  138

WHISKY SPEAK 152
FURTHER READING 156
INDEX 158
ACKNOWLEDGEMENTS 160

# INTRODUCTION

The first time I ever drank whisky I was almost too young to know better. Things ended badly. My grandma had to rescue me. I wouldn't touch a drop of the stuff until a few years ago, on a press trip to Iceland. Bizarrely enough, we were there to taste a rare 45-year-old single malt whisky, the Dalmore Aurora, named after the aurora borealis – the northern lights.

Save its name, there is no good reason why we should have been drinking it in Iceland. But we were, and if I was at the time a tad bewildered by the fuss, nobody else was. The whisky itself had been flown in separately, a week prior to our arrival, where it had sat in pride of place at the Hotel Rangá, rumours of its presence attracting a steady stream of pilgrims. The idea had been that we would taste beneath the lights, but it was April, the tail end of the season, and it was cloudy. We drank indoors. No matter. The Dalmore Aurora didn't need a light show. It was quite a revelation – in its own right.

Apart from being amazed that it tasted nothing like I remembered whisky tasting, I was perplexed by the fact that it was spicy, and tasted of caramel. I couldn't care less that it was just one of 200 bottles in the world – or that each went for £3000 a pop. I wanted to know why something consisting largely of ethanol and water should end up brown, light, sharp and slightly sweet, and why some of the group smelt pear and apple, melon, burnt marmalade, while others found roses, jasmine and chocolate. I liked that it had been distilled in stills nicknamed 'the fat bastards', but I had no idea how the bastards worked, nor the import of words like ex-bourbon, American white or Matusalem.

I wanted to know what all these words meant. I wanted to know why a liquid should smell and taste of things that it was patently not made of. I was yet to learn about the making of flavour, the effect of copper, the influence of wood, but I sensed a science behind the magic.

THIS BOOK IS THE RESULT OF THAT SENSING. IT'S SHORT – short enough to be read in one sitting. It's designed to give you a good working knowledge of whisky, its production, various histories, its styles and types, an idea of what to drink. It's comprehensive, but it's not deep. The whiskies mentioned here are all findable and largely, I'd like to say, affordable, but that would be your call. This is a light journey, touching on many things. It's a stepping stone, a means of going from knowing something to knowing something more to wanting to know something else.

To which end, if you have a bottle of whisky to hand, pour yourself a drink. If not, then it's up to you, but I would be tempted to pop down to your local bar. It doesn't really matter, but I'm hoping that, like my experience in Iceland, you know very little about how that liquid in your glass came to be what it is. Smell it. Take a sip. Take another. Now, start reading. And enjoy. I promise not to bore – though I must now break that promise with some history, definitions, terms and arbitrary decision making.

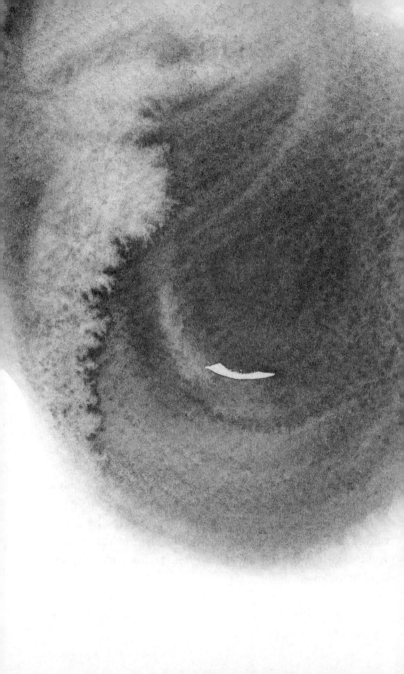

# 1 IN THE NAME
OF WHISKY

A whisky is defined as a spirit made from a cereal mixed with water, mashed and fermented to make a distiller's beer, which is then distilled and aged.

## THE BIRTH OF WHISKY

Nobody can say for sure who first thought that distilling beer might be a good idea. There is some evidence that points to distillation being as old as ancient Egypt, where it was more than likely used for the purpose of making perfume. Certainly, the art of 'purification' was well known to Persian alchemists, and their works were translated into Latin as early as the twelfth century. It's generally thought, however, that beer distilled to be drunk as a medicine or restorative, so-called aqua vitae or 'water of life', was the work of well-travelled Irish monks, having learnt the trade during lengthy stays in the Moorish courts of Spain. From Ireland it is supposed that the court physicians or *ollamhs* – such as the MacBeathads, in the service of Aine O'Cathain – would have carried the knowledge east, onto the island kingdoms of the Hebrides, from which it eventually spread to mainland Scotland.

Most of which we can't really prove: while there are early hints as to its use in Ireland, with soldiers reported to have fortified themselves with shots of 'uisce beatha' (aqua vitae), the first primary evidence, as whisky writer Dave Broom notes, of beer being actually distilled in Britain is to be found in Chaucer's *Canterbury Tales*. We wait another century, though, for actual written mention of aqua vitae being made in the world of non-fiction, a line in the King James IV Exchequer Rolls, which reports the activities of one Brother John Cor, who goes down in most historians' books as being the world's first whisky distiller.

Common sense says otherwise – as we shall see. At any rate, the whisky being made at this time – and for much of the rest of its history – was drunk straight off the stills, either in its raw state, or having been flavoured during distillation, or once flavoured post-distillation. In this sense, it was more a type of vodka or gin than the brown spirit we know today. For that, we would have to wait until the nineteenth century, when spirit stored in oak storage casks was found not only to have turned red, but also to taste better, especially that which had ended up in ex-sherry casks or in ones whose innards had been sanitised by firing.

## WHISKY OR WHISKEY?

The Americans and the Irish spell whisky with an 'e'; the rest of the world does not. This simple division is slightly complicated by the fact that a minority of American producers choose to spell it without the 'e', citing either difference or Old World authenticity as good reason, which isn't necessarily true, but no big deal.

However, for writers, journalists and authors, unless actually quoting 'whisky' or 'whiskey' as in its use as a proper name – the 'Teeling Irish Whiskey Company', for example – then the word ought to be spelt consistently, either with or without an 'e'.

In other words, rather than follow publications' style guides, which generally follow country leads when it comes to spelling 'whisky', better that the whisky writer follow the standardised spelling system used by the country in which he or she is writing and publishing. It's logical, therefore, and not at all disrespectful, that I should spell 'whisky' without the 'e', given that I write in British English.

While speaking of logic, unless standing for a place or name, or as part of a title, 'scotch' and 'bourbon' begin here in lower case, as does 'sherry', 'cognac' or any other common noun. The only time 'scotch' is 'Scotch' is when it is used in place of the word Scottish – as in 'Scotch whisky'. Please, you may now take a long sip of that drink.

## MEASURING POWER

The strength of a whisky is measured in alcohol by volume or abv. By this is meant the percentage of ethanol in a given volume of whisky. While a spirit in general may be defined as being 20% abv or above, a whisky must start at 40%. It's a universally understood measure, though many an American maker and drinker will also measure in 'proof', a historical corruption of the word 'proved', as in how sailors used to pour a portion of their rum rations onto gunpowder and set it alight so as to 'prove' the strength of their liquid pay cheques. In America, a proof is simply double the abv – for example, 100 proof is 50% abv.

## MAIN STYLES

There are four recognised styles of whisky: malt, grain, Irish pot still and bourbon. Each of these four distinct whisky styles can be said to possess its own overarching set of flavour traits, though – like wine, like cognac, like anything to do with flavour – any whisky, whatever its style, can be usefully broken into four generic taste descriptors, the most commonly employed being variations on 'light', 'rich', 'delicate' and 'smoky', these being terms favoured by Dave Broom and Diageo's influential *The Flavour Map*™.

Further, very few whiskies are adequately categorised as simply light, rich, delicate or smoky. Where one is the opposite of the other, so a whisky can be anything from very light to extremely rich, from fragilely delicate to unbelievably smoky – and more than likely fall into at least two of our generic categories, which in turn subdivide into further subsets of flavour descriptors. Warning: whisky – it's complicated.

## TENNESSEE WHISKY

A possible sub-style: in America, a Tennessee whisky is federally defined as a 'straight bourbon whiskey authorised to be produced in the State of Tennessee', a distinction clarified at state level as being a bourbon that has also undergone the Lincoln County Process – that is, the spirit is put through a maple charcoal filter before being laid down to age. To make things even more difficult for you to follow, the state has allowed the Benjamin Pritchard Distillery special dispensation, exempting it from the ruling. Thus are all Benjamin Pritchard products labelled 'Tennessee whiskey', even though they do not use the process that defines Tennessee whisky as Tennessee whisky. I have saved you the trouble of having to think any more about this: when I say bourbon I mean Tennessee whisky too.

## MALT WHISKY

A malt whisky is made with primarily malted grain, nearly always distilled in pot stills, and is generally matured in ex-bourbon or ex-sherry oak casks. Most of the world's malts are made with malted barley, a significant minority of which are peated. As a style, malt whisky making was born in Scotland and Ireland, having evolved from beer-making traditions, was imported wholesale by Japan and latterly by Taiwan, and is practised to a much lesser degree throughout the rest of the world.

Flavour-wise, a malted whisky is generally understood as falling into one of five zones or camps: fragrant and floral; dry and malty; fruity and spicy; rich and round; and smoky and peaty. Why one or two and not the others will depend on a whole range of production variables: the malting and possible peating of the grain, the length of mash and fermentations, the choice of yeast, the type of stills employed, the methods used during distillation, the spirit's strength, the type of oak used to mature it, the size, age and possible previous use of the cask along with the quality of maturation. In a nutshell, everything – people included.

## BOURBON

As with single malt whiskies, bourbon falls into several flavour camps. Always a 'mash' of at least 51% corn, and nearly always flavoured with a so-called 'small' grain, usually rye, but also wheat, a bourbon may be one or more of many tasty things: sometimes light and fragrant; more often fruity and spicy; frequently rich and bold; occasionally smoky.

However, it's just as fair to say, when speaking of a recognisable flavour profile, that every bourbon will inevitably share a similar set of vital statistics. In the first place, it's generally sweeter than a malt whisky, its taste a litany of creamy caramels, of toffee, butterscotch and maple syrup. Second, it's run through with vanillas, with the scent of new wood, of pine, sap or bark, and marked by hints of coconut, of suntan oil, the taste of stewed apple. We examine the whys and wherefores of this later.

Further variations on the profile fall into two camps: rye and wheat. If a bourbon is flavoured with rye, then add pepper and spice to the corn, a citrus-like sharpness to the finish, the pleasant irritation of something like eucalyptus, menthol or cloves. If flavoured with wheat, then it's a weightlifter in silken slippers, the creamy mouthfeel of corn augmented by the taste of nuts, the fragrance of honey, the delicacy of wild flowers.

## IRISH POT STILL WHISKY

The uniqueness of the flavours of Irish pot still whisky is to be found in the fact it is always made from a mix of both unmalted and malted barley, and that it is traditionally and usually triple distilled.

While the influence of the malt will be similar to that found in single malt whiskies, the unmalted barley gives Irish pot still whisky its slightly oilier, more acidic, spicier, big mouthfeel flavour profile. Meanwhile, the extra distillation makes for higher alcohol content, the distilled spirit or 'new make' rendered lighter, less heavily flavoured, much sweeter.

All of which means a super-complex whisky, the ratio of malted to unmalted determining the extent to which those flavours distinct to barley make it through to the wood, the influence of which will depend on oak type and cask age: a re-charred ex-bourbon first-fill will add vanillas, caramels, coconut and soft fruits; a similarly aged ex-sherry cask will bring extra tannins, possible greater richness, the smell and taste of dried fruits, spices and tobacco.

## GRAIN WHISKY

Grain is the last great and relatively undiscovered bastion of whisky – really more neglected than undiscovered. All whisky, of course, is made from grain, but grain whisky is legally defined as an actual style in Scotland, Ireland and Japan. Constituting a minority portion of malted barley and a majority of unmalted grain(s), usually wheat or maize, it is distilled through a continuous or column still, taken off at very high strength, and has traditionally been put to the service of creating blends, especially in Scotland.

Given its blending role, historically speaking, very little grain has been bottled in and of itself, the thinking being that while perfectly suited to the task of giving a quality of lightness, volume and sweetness to a blend, the average grain whisky lacks enough flavour to qualify as being a whisky worth drinking in its own right. As said, times are a changing, with some very fine releases showing that, when paired to the right cask, it's more than capable of ending up delicious.

## A FOOTNOTE OF CAVEATS

I've had a crack at Tennessee whisky, it being more or less a bourbon, but in the world of whisky the problem of categorisation is more than a single state-sized thorn. There are country-specific problems, with legislators having either nannied whisky types into almost nonsensical categories, or having been so laissez-faire as to have neglected to properly clothe and feed their own. However, the uber-problem here is the fact that the four styles do not adequately cover every whisky out there.

Examples: by definition an American rye whisky is almost everything that a bourbon is, except the big and small grains are reversed. A corn whisky is a grain whisky, except that it can be made in a pot still. Many Canadian whiskies fall across several styles and types of whisky. None can be fairly defined as being any one set style, the various regulations cancelling each other out. Indeed, thinking on styles, there's no real reason why – except legal – bourbon might not be better understood as a subset of grain. This is more than confusing. It's crazy. Take another sip.

That's the first issue, and one which could be solved by going back to the definitions board. The second, however, is much more about the quantum-like impossibility of pinning down flavour. Meaning, while it is fine and perfectly reasonable to talk about the four styles having specific flavour profiles, and these breaking down into recognisable flavour subsets, taste three same style whiskies against each other – three malts, for example – and what do you get? The same and the different, all in one go. They're whisky, they're malt, and they're the product of their own distilleries, the many variables that constitute their making, people very much included.

Third and finally, whatever our knowledge, our technical knowhow, whisky making remains an imprecise science. Long may it continue. We may have our styles, our set methods, but we're not making cans of beans. There are those in the whisky -making business who can speak in molecular strings, others who will tell you why spectrometry is God's gift to maturation, and still those for whom the word syringaldehyde is a picture of flavours, and yet all would agree: nothing is certain. Whatever our styles, our predilection for categorising nomenclatures, whisky making remains a thing beholden to the magic of science and to the science of magic.

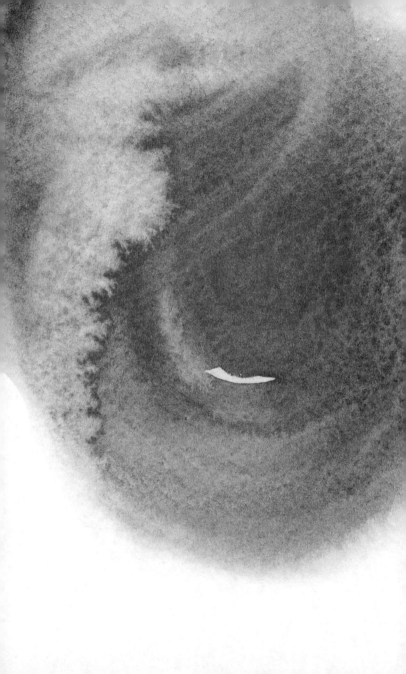

# 2 FROM GRAIN TO GLASS

Knowledge is not necessary to pleasure. Knowing how a record is manufactured does not make us better dancers. We do not need to know how to write a novel to enjoy one. Understanding how whisky is made does not magically make it taste better. If you were to give this chapter a miss, you would be none the worse for not knowing the technicalities of whisky production. Indeed, the word itself – production – is enough to put anyone off wanting to know anything about how we manage the apparent miracle of converting a cereal into the world's most complex drink. It sounds like school and those geography lessons that weren't about volcanoes.

However, while knowing how barley is malted – or why we extract starch from corn, or the meaning of a wash still, or wherefore the Angel's Share – has next to no negative effect on our capacity for enjoying a dram, the story of how the contents of the glass in your hand got to be here is an extraordinary one. It sees a grain – normally malted barley, corn, rye or wheat – turned into beer, which is distilled and then aged in wood. It's a special thing.

## MALTING THE BARLEY

Any grain destined for the making of a malted whisky needs malting first. Traditionally and usually, this would be barley, which is valued for its starch-to-sugar converting enzymes. These are activated via the barley's malting, a process that involves fooling the presently dormant grain into beginning to sprout.

While the same kind of enzymes occur naturally in other germinating grains, none are as effective as those produced by barley, which is why the mix of grains or 'mashbill' used for nearly all other whiskies will contain a small portion of malted barley.

## STARCH TO SUGAR

Visit the average distillery and more than likely the first port of call will be the grist mill. A retro-beast of a machine, its job is to grind by hammer or roller the grain kernels and so allow for subsequent extraction of their sugars, after which the grist – the husks, flour and in-betweens – is then either mixed with hot water or actually cooked, like a soup.

Given the fact of its malting, which has already started the job of turning the starch into sugar, barley marked for the making of malt or Irish pot whiskies does not require cooking, and instead the grist is mixed or 'mashed' in a pot-shaped vessel known as the mash tun. The increasingly hot waters dissolve the sugars and so separate them from the barley solids, the best of which – the 'wort' – is drained off in preparation for fermentation.

Other grains, their starch that bit more protected, require cooking – under pressure or in enormous open tubs. As a rule of thumb, the base grain – normally wheat, corn or rye – is cooked until its starch content is suitably hydrolysed. If a single grain mash, the temperature is then lowered, the malted barley added and time allowed for the conversion of the grain's starch to sugar. If a mixed grain style, such as is bourbon, the temperature is adjusted to accommodate the addition of the so-called flavour grain, either rye or wheat, before adding the malted barley.

In the making of bourbon and grain whiskies, the solids are not separated off from the sugary liquid, and so the 'mash' remains a part of the process right up until distillation.

## SUGAR TO ALCOHOL

Once mashed, the resulting wort or mash is cooled and then pumped into fermentation vats or 'washbacks'. Traditionally made of wood, but more often now of stainless steel, especially in large facilities, and reminiscent of giant covered milk pails or buckets, it is here that the sugar is converted into alcohol.

The catalyst for the change is distiller's yeast, which when pitched has the effect of, first, using up the oxygen, a frenetic and wickedly smelly process, and then, having run out, switching to living off the sugar, with alcohol being its main by-product.

Depending on the distiller's approach, fermentation lasts from anything between 50 and 120 hours, and is pretty much the same the world over, except that in the case of the making of most bourbon whiskies, where the water is hard, the process includes adding back a portion of the previous day's mash.

Known variously as 'setback' or 'backset', this 'spent mash' is high in acids, and so doubles up as both ironer out of pH scales and natural antiseptic.

Thus is beer made – less the hops. The wort or mash has now become a 'wash'. If it's destined to be a bourbon, then it's 5–6% abv strength. If a malt, it'll come in at 8–9% abv. The rest is water. Next stop: distillation.

## CONCENTRATING THE BEER

Distillation is an old and simple practice: the wash is heated. The alcohol content, which evaporates at a lower temperature than water, vaporises first, and is then subsequently recaptured as it condenses back to liquid.

Do it once and the alcoholic strength of the resultant 'low wines' averages out at about 23% abv, at which point it is by definition a spirit, albeit a very weak one. Do it twice and the so-called 'new make' comes off the stills at between 68–71% abv (or at around 94.5% abv if a grain whisky). If triple distilled, as in the case of Irish pot still and a small number of single malt whiskies, it is somewhere in the eighties, depending on the distillery.

Today, and depending on grain type and individual approach, a distillery will use one or both of two types of still: pot or column. The pot still is the most traditional, and mandatory for the production of malt whisky in Scotland,

## POT vs COLUMN STILLS

Made of copper, the pot still is topped by a long neck and a lyne arm, which runs into a condenser. Imagine a swan, its upper torso, neck and head, something stuck on the end of its beak. Some are squat and ungainly looking, some tall and elegant.

The wash pot is filled with the new (usually all liquid) wash. Heated either by direct fire or steam, it's brought to the boil, the vapours rising up the neck, flowing down or up the lyne arm and into the condenser, whereupon they are gradually turned back into liquid, and collected into a new wines vat. The process is then repeated through the spirits still and in a more refined way, one that sees the liquid separated or cut into three parts: foreshorts, middle and feints. The foreshorts and feints are the unwanted parts of the distillate. The middle part is what the distiller is after, and he or she will cut this according to flavour and character. The new make batch is then pumped into a spirits receiver, the whole process taking between 10 and 16 hours.

The column still goes about the business of distilling beer in a radically different way. Composed of a (normally multi-storey high) stainless steel tube and separated internally by a series of plates, the mash or beer is pumped in close to the top of the column, while steam rises up through the bottom, heating the plates. As the beer hits the plates, which get progressively hotter the further it descends, so the alcohol is vaporised and carried off into a second condensing column, where it is passed up through copper plates. These so-called rectifying plates constantly re-condense heavier gas compounds, allowing only the lightest of vapours to the top, where finally they condense into the new make. In comparison to the pot still, the column still functions continuously and distils at a much higher ratio of alcohol to water, creating a lighter style distillate.

while the column still, also known also as the continuous or Coffey still, was first properly introduced to the industry by Robert Stein (in 1825), improved on by Aeneas Coffey (in 1834), and widely adopted by grain whisky producers thereafter. Owing to the fact of the beer being distilled twice (sometimes three times, very occasionally more), stills generally come in pairs: the larger wash still and the low wines or spirits still.

If a combination of the column and the pot is used, the beer still is usually – in America – used to both strip and rectify the alcohol, while the pot further refines. In Canada the column is used for the production of the low wines, the pot reserved for the flavouring spirit.

## FROM NEW MAKE TO NEW WHISKY

The new make taken off the stills, the batch is then usually diluted to strength (62.5–63.5% abv) and filled into oak casks.

The rudiments of the whisky cask are the same whatever the type or size. Fashioned from oak staves, they are what is known as tight (liquid holding) casks and show nothing as much as a nail or tack between them. The standard two casks used are the American Standard Barrel (bourbon) and the slightly larger hogshead (Irish and Scottish). Others include the once ubiquitous sherry butt, whisky octaves, small gallon barrels, quarter casks, barriques, port pipes, Madeira and the puncheon. The vast majority are made from American white, European, French or Japanese oak.

The filled casks are transported for storage to warehouses – either on or off site. Here they reside for years, intermittently monitored by the distiller or the warehouse manager.

Once deemed ready, and unless destined to be a single cask bottling, the mature whisky is then vatted or blended with more of itself – different casks and batches of the same whisky from the same distillery, some of which may well be older than it is.

## MARRY, FILTER, COLOUR, BOTTLE

After blending, there are – depending on tradition, the law and interest – a number of options before bottling.

Whatever the nature of the style, once it's been dumped and – unless cask strength – diluted to strength, the distiller may choose to 'marry' the whisky, by which is meant giving the now blended batches time to settle, to get to know each other, generally in large exhausted casks, and for between three and six months. Further, in order to stop the whisky clouding, which it naturally does when at low temperatures and below 46% abv, a whisky can be chill-filtered. Finally, caramel may be used as a colour agent. (Note: both chill-filtering and colouring are a hot topic, being considered by some producers to spoil the natural taste of the whisky.)

Once ready, the whisky is bottled, capped and labelled – sometimes on site, more often off. Either that or it is sold on or swapped for the purpose of being blended with other whiskies.

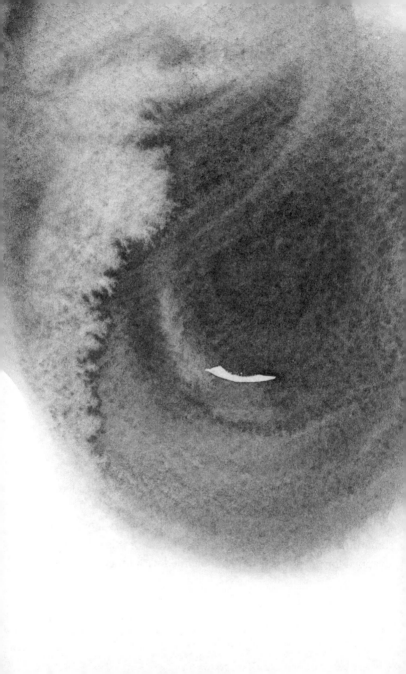

# 3

## THE ART OF
## THE DISTILLER

Whisky making is not about following a formula. It's about creating a whisky full of character and flavour. It's about recipe and how it's worked, interpreted, played with. It's about maths and science, yes, but also it's about accident and surprise, about intuition, feel and flow. Elemental and natural, yet technological and crafted, it is a sometimes heated, occasionally languid, and often drawn-out conversation between grain, water, copper and wood, as facilitated by the distiller, and by the world of the distillery itself.

## MAKES AND FLAVOURS

Distillers have known for long before science began to explain why that the distillate or 'new make' is not, in the truest sense, a neutral spirit, that it holds flavour, and that the type and extent of that flavour depends on some or all of the choices made at key stages of the process. We're making a spirit that tastes of the distillery that gave birth to it. That's personality.

In the first instance, such a personality begins with the grain. As well as possessing their own specific taste profiles (*see* pages 34–35), grains are deliberately imbued with flavours, all of which are designed to survive and influence the fermentation and distillation processes. To this end, a distiller may roast or peat the grain. Owing to the reductive effect it has on starch levels, and therefore on yield of alcohol, roasting is reasonably rare: in terms of how it enhances flavour, it's all in the name. Peating, meanwhile, is practised in the making of some malt whiskies, and as such is a fine example of necessity being the mother, with the decomposed vegetation that makes up peat bogs all that was available when it came to finding fuel to burn and so dry out the malt. The science behind the effect unbeknown to early maltsters, peat smoke ('reek') contains vaporised oils, certain chemicals (phenols) of which re-solidify on contact with the husks of the still damp, malting barley. The process gives the final whisky its characteristic smoky overtones.

This deepening and developing of personality continues on through the mash and into fermentation, the magic that sees sugar converted to alcohol being also a magic that is all about the creation of flavour. As well as making ethanol, which has no flavour, fermentation gives birth to various hyper-powerful flavour compounds or 'cogeners', of which there are four main types: acids, esters, aldehydes and higher alcohols. Mere trace elements, these cogeners are formed at various stages of the fermentation, and are responsible for the wash's overall fruity flavour. The shorter the fermentation, the more cereal notes carry through to the wash. The longer and cooler the run, the fruitier it gets, the caveat being that the tail end of the process is vulnerable to bacterial growth, some good, some not so good. Further, sulphury flavours are as much a by-product of fermentation as fruit esters, and can, if allowed, taint the wash. A select few are desirable; all are not.

## THE FLAVOURS OF GRAINS

Each of the four main whisky-making grains comes with its own unique bundle of flavours.

Generally speaking, malted barley will give the new make a biscuit-like taste, a soft-baked depth that will, if allowed, survive into and be complemented by maturation. Unmalted barley, meanwhile, comes over as all peppery and oily and sharp fruit. Corn is sweeter than barley, its high starch content translating as a bass-like fatness. Rye is the devil in a bespoke tweed suit, a hot citrus-based chutney in hand-stitched boots. Wheat's the boxer of the bunch, beautiful and intelligent, light and honey-footed, its punch well-executed, not an ounce of wasted energy. As well as the four main whisky-making grains, other grains variously and occasionally used include spelt, millet and oats – so-called pseudograins like buckwheat and quinoa too. All impart their own specific flavours.

As well as sourcing different types of grain, a growing number of distillers swear by individual varieties, arguing for flavour over yield. When mixed, and at different ratios, the grains create new flavours. The different mashbills used in the making of bourbon are a perfect example of this. A bourbon mashbill consists of a majority portion of corn, a percentage of normally rye and about 10% malted barley. In some bourbons, the rye is substituted for wheat. If a 'high rye' bourbon, then the spice is very evident, though the quality of the making means the corn's weight ought to balance and soften the fire. If low, then the bite's much more subtle, the corn's sweet butter-like fullness welling up beneath. If a wheated bourbon, think light, smooth, honey, the corn a double sugar hit.

Some distillers are happy to share their mashbill ratios, others are not!

## THE ALCHEMY OF COPPER

The jury's out as to whether copper actually creates flavours, with some arguing for its role in the appearance of certain unseen esters. No doubt, however, as to the efficacy of copper's ability to strip, through direct contact with its vapours, the spirit of heavier and usually unwanted flavours – sulphuric, meaty and, to a lesser extent, feinty notes.

In this respect, the longer the contact between copper and vapour, the lighter and more elegant the spirit; the shorter the contact, the heavier and more endowed with character it is. Think flowers and perfumed oils versus sulphur and meat. The shape, design and use of the stills help decide the length of contact, and therefore the character of the spirit.

## CUTTING TO TASTE

Whatever the grain and how it's been treated, whatever the success of the creation of new flavours during the mashing and fermentation processes, I can't stress enough how easy it is for a distiller to lose, destroy or taint flavour during distillation.

Most of the spirit run – its head and tails, or foreshots and feints – is either poisonous or foul-tasting, and will be recycled back into the next wash. The size of middle of the run, the part worth holding onto, will depend entirely on the distiller and what kind of whisky he or she is after. Cogeners are very well-behaved. They respond to temperature, and vaporise in a set and strict order: lightest first, heaviest last. The lightest are very floral, grassy and green. The middleweights are all fruits, the lightest of these crisp and fresh, the heaviest red, soft, ripe and even stewed. As the heaviest cogeners come into play, so the fruit almost rots off, making way for cereal and smoke, the oils and tar.

Which of these the distiller picks, and which he or she lets go, will depend on flavour objectives. An early first cut picks up the flowers; a late first cut, more fruit than flower. If looking for flower and fruit, but steering clear of the heavies, then the second cut needs to be made before the appearance of the smoke. If after a full-blooded fruit with plenty of smoke, then it's a cut towards the middle and a late finish. If after the whole spectrum, then early and late, though with great care – a feinty-tasting new make is a potentially off-tasting whisky.

Crucially, the run decreases in levels of ethanol. More ethanol means fewer flavour cogeners. The earlier the cuts, therefore, the higher the new make's level of alcohol content, and so the less it will retain flavours gained in the mash and during fermentation.

## THE MIRACLE OF OAK

However important it is in terms of contributing to flavour, it is during its years spent in wood that the new make actually becomes a whisky. Many a distiller believes oak – almost always oak – contributes to 70% of the final article, its flavour, its balance, its overall structure.

Hear this: in the land of flavour making, the cask is king, its position earned for the extraordinary role it plays in maturing the distillate, which it does either by adding or removing flavours in three distinct ways: extraction, evaporation and reaction.

The spirit in a barrel is never still. Rising ambient temperatures cause the liquid to expand, pushing into the wood, variously dissolving and decomposing its sugars, tannins and simple flavour compounds. As ambient temperatures decrease, so the spirit turns in on itself, contracts, and draws or extracts the wood's caramels, colouring and flavour compounds into itself. Expanding and contracting – year in, year out – the spirit rhythmically feasts on the barrel, though most fiercely in the first year.

At the same time, changes brought on by this interaction with the wood are compounded and aided by the process of evaporation, a phenomenon popularly known as the Angel's Share, with sharp- and bitter-tasting sulphides expelled suddenly, in the first month, and then gradually over time. The exiting gas is replaced by fresh oxygen, which acts as vital catalyst for the oxidation of ethanol into further flavour making chemical reactions. In this way, barrels can be said to breathe – through gaps in the joins and the bung hole.

Finally, as time passes, facilitated by oxygen, water and ethanol, a complex chain of reactions will occur between various wood chemicals in themselves, between the certain wood and spirit chemicals, and between specific components of the spirit itself, all of which eventually amounts to sour, off-smelling aldehydes turning into more pleasant acids, which in turn are converted into a range of flavoursome fruity esters, the final outcome being, hopefully, a deep and finely balanced package of flavours.

## YOUR CASK, SIR

Distillers' approach to wood source, to the cooperage and lifespan of a cask, borders on the manic obsessive. Today, whisky casks are a made-to-order phenomenon.

It's a mania that takes many forms, from tracking the oak from source to final cask, to insisting on the wood from a particular part of the tree, to most precisely selecting the tightness of grain, but the most radical piece of cask tailoring will be the decision as to whether to toast or char, or both – and at what level.

Toasting and charring are the application of thermal heat to the layers of the wood on the inside of the barrel, thereby breaking down its structure and creating flavours that are released into the spirit during the early stages of maturation. Toasting is as it sounds: toasting. It is not direct fire and lasts 15–45 minutes, at temperatures of between 100 and 200°C. Charring, meanwhile, is toasting gone spectacularly wrong. It's direct. It's much hotter. The barrel's innards are actually set alight, for a matter of seconds, the result a charred surface, black and pitted like a crocodile's skin. However, despite the extra heat, there's less penetration than a toast – think of the difference between burning and toasting a piece of bread.

## THE FLAVOURS OF OAKS

As with grain, so the type of oak chosen will help determine certain flavour profiles. Depending on length and quality of the maturation phase, American white, the most commonly used oak, gives its whiskies the taste of vanilla and coconut, of honey and toffee, of red fruits, ginger, almonds, the scent, eventually, of tobacco and leather. If European oak, then there's lots of tannin, of fruit cake, of cinnamon, clove, caramelised orange, the rich smells of a kitchen come Christmas pudding time. French oak, meanwhile, is similar, though imparts extra spice, while the much rarer Japanese oak, as well as inhabiting a cross-section of the above, comes with a whole bunch of extra acid fruits, as well as an added incense-like spiciness.

Before being made up into casks, all oak needs drying out or seasoning. Properly seasoned wood makes a real difference to flavour. Yard drying oak takes years, and happens outside. Exposed to the vagaries of season and weather, rot sets in, the various and successive colonies of fungi that make the wood their home taking root, and with it the formation of hydrogen peroxide, which as your hairdresser will tell you is a catalyst for chemical change, the sum of which, in the case of oak, serves to soften the tannins and unlock the wood's sugars.

The overall effect of both reduces tannins, and therefore tightness of mouthfeel in the whisky. It also caramelises sugars and releases vanillin. The charred layer has the added effect of filtering impurities during maturation, while the extra heat is enough to generate the appearance of various phenols, especially clove-like aromas and notes of smoke.

Depending on his or her strength of new make, on the degree of filter required, on the depth the wood needs penetrating, a distiller can opt for a light, medium or heavy toast, and for one of at least five grades of char. There's a lot to think about.

## WORK THAT CASK

Whatever the type of oak, a virgin cask makes for an immediate and powerful wood influence. If, therefore, like bourbon makers, legally committed to always using new casks, a distiller may either take the spirit off the stills at a lower strength or dilute the barrel entry strength – in order to slow down the rate of extraction. By the same token, a distiller may use a fresh cask to flush more tannin, or a certain sweetness, or vanillas, into a bull of a spirit.

Meanwhile, a used cask – ex-bourbon, sherry, cognac or wine – is valued for how the original liquid's years of interaction with wood will influence the taste of the distillate, and for the fact that the strength of influence of the used wood diminishes significantly with every reuse – perfect, then, for fragile, light spirits, which would otherwise be overwhelmed by the wood.

Distillers may then choose to move the spirit into different casks, either as a means of nursing a poorly maturing whisky along or in search of more flavour. As is increasingly the case, a distiller might choose to 'finish' a nearly matured whisky in a different type of used cask. Thus an ex-bourbon cask matured whisky will get a finish in a sherry butt, or in a wine cask, or a port pipe, the aim being to give the whisky a final layering of flavour, an element of character that it will not have got from the previous cask.

## DANCING WITH ANGELS

If indeed the cask is king, then its palace is the warehouse, and one that has enormous impact on rates of maturation – and therefore on flavour. It's an ageing tool in its own right.

### DUNNAGE OR RACKED

There are two main types of warehouse: dunnage and racked. The dunnage warehouse is the romantic's version of what a warehouse looks like, the racked a beancounter's ledger, a place where function rules. Actually, they're both beautiful, the former damp and low, sweet-smelling and dark, the latter, however financially expedient, paying unexpected homage to the architecture of the industrial revolution, styles that have over the years acquired a certain brutal grace – dark and silent halls, cathedrals of liquid gold.

## ANGEL'S SHARE

In deciding on cask type, its particular levels of customisation, as well as on what strength to barrel at, the distiller needs to account for the effects of temperature and humidity on annual rates of evaporation. The angels will have their share, though how big, and exactly what the nature of their tipple, will depend not only where in the world the cask is stored, but also its spot in the warehouse.

A cask, then, can lose on average anything from 2–12% of its liquid annually to evaporation. In maritime climates like Scotland or Ireland, where temperatures are low and humidity is high, the loss is more in alcohol than water. The reverse is true of hot, dry countries.

There's more. Individual warehouses come with their own microclimates, whereby ambient conditions – temperature, light, airflow and humidity – are affected by position and height, and by the materials the warehouse is made of. Easier to manage, the single-floor dunnage warehouse is less variable in terms of how it influences maturation.

By contrast, the ambient conditions of a racked warehouse will vary between the first and the twelfth rack, and considerably more between the ground and top floors, a factor well understood by distillers and warehouse managers, who speak of sweet spots, strength fill casks according to loss prediction and operate warehouse policies that rotate casks through the levels, or favour different warehouses for different whiskies.

There are attic angels and there are ground floor angels and there are many angels in between. The distiller must dance with them all.

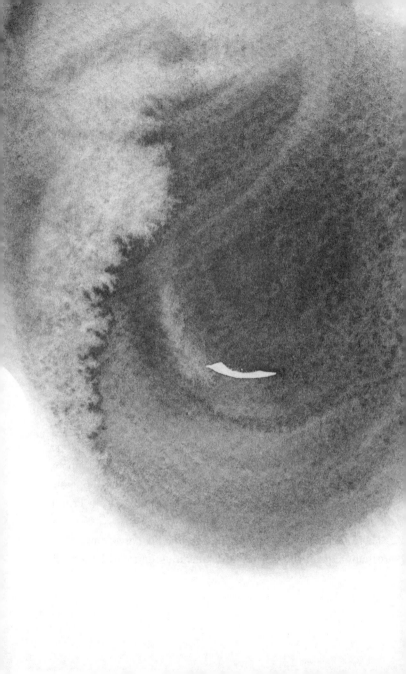

# 4

## MASTER OF
## THE BLEND

Whisky almost everywhere is usually one or more of two types of blend: first, it is nearly always the blend of different casks and batches of casks of the same whisky; second, it may also then be further blended with different whiskies. The former would be a bourbon, a single grain, a single malt or an Irish pot still whisky. The latter takes many forms, but is normally and officially known as a 'blended whisky'.

## AN UNFEASIBLY LARGE CURRY

The task of the distiller – or in the case of large operations, the master blender and his or her tasting panel – is hardly finished once the wood and warehouse have had their way. In order to produce enough of a specific brand, and to ensure a uniformity of flavour, different casks or batches of the matured whisky are mixed or blended together. This is a perfectly normal and overwhelmingly usual practice, but can seem to the outsider a tad confusing, given that some whiskies are labelled as blended and some are not. Let me explain – by way of a cooking analogy.

Imagine every week throwing a wonderful dinner party. Every Saturday you make the same curry, taken from a single recipe. Only, given your excellent cooking, you no longer have a pot large enough to feed your growing party of guests, so you end up making multiple batches, throughout the week, freezing them, then, on the big day, defrosting and mixing them together. In doing so you've achieved one of your aims, which is to ensure that there's enough to go round.

However, you have a problem. Your guests are an old bunch of friends who have come to love a specific curry, and want it to taste exactly the same every dinner party. In order to ensure that they get what they want, you follow the recipe slavishly, doing your level best to source the same ingredients. You test-taste each new batch against a batch kept over from the last dinner party. You discard any batch that's either too strong or different and that you think might spoil or alter the final curry's taste. Some of the new batches may be different, but not so much as to threaten the final taste, and these you portion off among the batches deemed ready. Only then do you mix the whole lot together.

The result: an unfeasibly large curry that tastes, you tell your guests, exactly the same as the unfeasibly large curry they all so enjoyed last week.

## THE HEGEMONY OF THE BRAND

As with your mythical curry, so the same of all whiskies, except of course those bottles whose contents are sourced exclusively from a single cask. Despite the distiller's best efforts, there is no guarantee that, say, two casks barrelled on the same day, from the same batch of new make, and aged for the same time, in the same spot in the warehouse, will produce whiskies with the same taste and character. You would think so, but whatever the variables foreseen, whatever the hypothesis, there will always be discernible differences.

In this respect, every barrel of whisky is unique, and as such a source of wonder if your interest as a producer or consumer is always the quality of difference, the joy of specialising in the one-off, the highlighting of an essential truth: that is, every barrel or batch of whisky is a physical moment in time, never to be repeated. This is the provenance of the independent bottler, the aficionado, the hunter, the collector, the super-enthusiast.

It is not, however, how distilleries generally make their money. Whether making malt, bourbon, grain or Irish pot still, the blender and his or her tasting panel will blend various barrels or batches of the same whisky in order to iron out perceived differences and so recreate a product considered exactly the same as all previous batches that went out bearing the self-same brand name – and enough of it to reach as much of the market as physically possible.

Of course, there is in all this a good bit of marketing guff. You may tell your guests that this week's curry tastes exactly the same as last week's, and the vast majority of the table would agree, unable to discern any differences, but analysed in a laboratory or tasted by a curry super-taster, previously indiscernible differences would begin to surface.

And if true of your curry, then even more so for whisky, which rather than sitting for a week in your freezer has spent perhaps decades maturing in wood. Owing to anything from a switch in grain varietal to unexpected changes in process to the tiny batch-by-batch differences in the oak sourced for ageing, a particular line will inevitably taste ever so slightly different, whatever the mastery of the blender. Thus, while imperceptible when set against, say, last year's release, when compared across the years, the differences become more and more apparent – in some cases, startlingly so. Enthusiasts love this sort of thing, and are right to call brands out on claims for the impossible.

## THE BONZA BLEND

A 'blended whisky' is a blend of two or more different whiskies, which brings me to the story of the Bonza Blend. In Australia, 'bonza' has various ultra-positive meanings – great, excellent, brilliant etc. – and 'beauty bonza' is reserved for verging-on-godly outcomes. The Bonza Blend is the name I gave to the first sample bottle of Scotch blended whisky I ever had a hand in making. It is also the last – and for good reason. I share the following piece of humiliation as a means of illustrating how very bloody hard it is to blend two or more whiskies.

The Glengoyne Distillery is one of Scotland's most beautiful distilleries. It's situated north of Glasgow, and considers itself the southernmost Highland distillery, its warehouses technically in the Lowlands. As well as operating long fermentation times and one of the slowest distillations in Scotland, Glengoyne hosts a fine tour, one which invariably ends with the opportunity not only to taste its wares, but also to have a go at making a blend of several different whiskies, hailing from all five of Scotland's whisky-making regions. It is here that the only bottle of Bonza Blend the world has ever known was born.

While I have no idea as to where exactly each of the whiskies came from, other than their regions, I remember enthusiastically matching the lighter, more floral-smelling whiskies with a touch of the heavier peated offerings, and being possessed of the belief that I was on the way to making a cracking blend. I think I blended seven whiskies, of different amounts, before writing, in my very best handwriting, 'Bonza Blend' on the label provided, dating and, I confess, even signing it. Revelling in the depths of my laboratory-fuelled fantasy, I think I thought I might be on to something.

Later, I presented the Bonza Blend to my wife, who took a sip, and made a face and many unprintable suggestions as to what I ought to do with it. I took the path of least painful resistance and put it in a kitchen cupboard, where it sits today, usually between a bag of flour and some tins of beans, a salutary reminder of my propensity for absolute vanity, and of the fact that blending whisky really is an art form, one that, like any art making, requires talent, knowing one's tools, a certain compulsive focus, and the willingness to practise, endlessly.

## TERMS OF AN ART

In Scotland, the blending of different whiskies results in one of three types of blends: 'blended malt', 'blended grain' and 'blended Scotch', the last of these – a blend of malt and grain – representing some 90% of Scotland's output. Unless prefaced by the word 'single', all scotches are blends made from whiskies sourced from two or more distilleries. Note: 'single' means single distillery, not single grain.

Ireland has a similar style, but is limited by distillery choice. Japan is also a producer of multi-distillery blends, if limited, like Ireland, by its relatively small number of producers, and also by a general reluctance (among distilleries) to trade styles – hence the likes of Suntory sourcing malt from abroad. Both Canada and Japan have developed single distilleries with the capacity to create different styles from which to create blends. If in Scotland, these would be called single blends, at which point we would need to call time on all whisky glossaries.

In the US, the majority of whisky is American straight whisky, meaning it is vatted batches of whisky made in a single distillery. An American blend, however, is altogether different, being a mix of a normally minority portion of straight whisky and a neutral unaged spirit – that is, vodka.

## ART OF THE BLEND

A well-blended whisky is a work of works. Like a perfumer combining perfumes, it's turning the unexpectedly new into the wanted old; or it's twisting a variety of the familiar into something unexpected, new or pleasantly different. Either way, the blend is a build, a splicing together of structures, tastes and characters, a work requiring an intelligence born of two polar opposites: a desire for chaos and a desire for order; a curiosity that revels in the knowledge that solutions are nothing without problems.

Obviously, when it comes to simply ensuring that a product adheres to a specific and already established profile, then the chaos – the fact that a given cask or batch tastes different, or that a whisky previously used can't be sourced – is righted as a matter of brand-conscious priority. Order – balance, harmony – is brought by the blender and his or her tasting panel, a task that might, for example, involve solving a batch's surprising dry, astringent mouthfeel by adding in whisky sourced from second or third fill casks.

However, when bringing balance to a blend of different styles of whiskies, such as in the case of a blended scotch, then the chaos or problem is more than just knowing the flavour profiles of the grain and malt whiskies you might choose to use. A blender understands, first, how a grain whisky's natural creamy sweetness informs – adapts, changes, smoothes – the malts; second, that it and its few fellows are both base and glue for the largely headstrong and skittish malts; and third, that the ratio of grains to malts might be in the region of one to eight, such is the former's subtle strength. The grain knits the malts together, and to itself, and in doing so, helps create something else – balance, harmony, a new order. Something, then, unlike the Bonza Blend, which was, is, and will always be a big old bottle of mess.

## OLD DOG, NEW TRICKS

If the blend as an enthusiast's whisky is once again on the up, then so also is the interest in those single malts originally made exclusively for blends. It's a real turn of events. The party line has long been that malts designed for blends are either not good enough or too specific to stand on their own two feet. Given this, the cynical view would be that the reasons for their sudden appearance are a matter of market economics: greater single malt consumption + rapidly depleted ageing stocks = release of whiskies previously deemed fit only for blends. Truth is, that's not wholly fair – on producers, consumers, blends or history. Every distillery possesses its own distinct personality. Some possess extraordinary character, character that has hitherto only been properly understood in relation to how the spirit they produce might fit with other whiskies. Given time, the odd tweak, a helping hand in the warehouse or in the quality of wood, a number have shown that they are more than capable of rolling out world class whiskies. Watch this space: this is just the beginning.

## FINE EXAMPLES

The below are blended Scotch and blended malt whiskies. Japanese and Irish blends appear under their relevant country sections (*see* pages 86–87 and 98–99). Where possible, the master blender responsible for the blends is namechecked in place of a single distillery.

**The Antiquary 12** (40%) (Signatory). Underrated and underexplored. Really lovely blended Scotch.

**Ballantine's 17** (43%) *Sandy Hyslop* (Chivas Bros–Pernod Ricard). Well known, long lived blend. Slow burn wonder.

**The Black Bull 12** (50%) *Euan Shand* (Duncan Taylor). An old blend revived. High grain content. Excellent.

**Black Grouse** (40%) *Gordon Motion* (Edrington Group). Entry level peated blended Scotch. Kind on the wallet and on the mouth. For a bigger kick try the Alpha. The Naked's good too.

**Blue Hanger** (45.6%) *Doug McIvor* (Berry Bros). Much vaunted and long-running series of blended malt whiskies. If you get the chance, drink it.

**Buchanan's Special Reserve 18** (43%) *Keith Law* (Diageo). Priceyish but worth it, as is much of the rest of the range.

**Cutty Sark 18** (43%) *Kirsteen Campbell* (Edrington Group). Very, very refined. The 12's also excellent.

**Dewar's 18** (43%) *Stephanie Macleod* (Bacardi). The grain's very much in charge here. Thick and beautiful.

**Haig Dimple 15** (40%) *Chris Clark* (Diageo). Sit with this. The US's Dimple Pinch. A proper classic.

**Hedonism** (43%) *John Glaser* (Compass Box). Really anything by irreverent and multi-talented Compass Box is a pleasure. This one's a blended grain.

**Johnnie Walker Black Label** (40%) *Jim Beveridge* (Diageo). Sit with this. Really good value peated blend. For something extra special, go blue.

**Mackinlay's The Journey** (47.3%) *Richard Paterson* (Whyte & Mackay–Emperador). Son of Discovery, Paterson's masterful recreation of the Shackleton whiskies.

**Naked Grouse** (40%) *Gordon Motion* (Edrington Group). Peaty blended Scotch. Kind on the wallet and on the mouth.

**Royal Salute 21** (43%) *Colin Scott* (Chivas Bros–Pernod Ricard). Power to the blend. A real masterpiece.

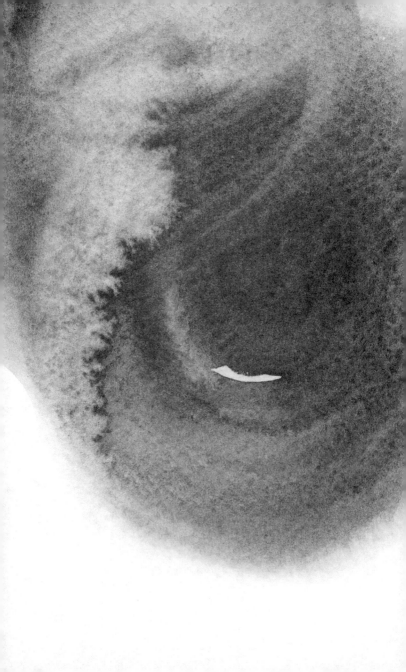

# 5

## SCOTLAND: THE LABYRINTH OF UISGE BEATHA

Owing to its highly successful marketing of an image clothed in kilt, bagpipe, mountain and stag, Scotland appears, from the outside, as unimaginably simple: it's the home of golf, the haggis and scotch. The romanticised touch points of a Scotland first dreamt up by the likes of Sir Walter Scott, it's an almost ahistorical take on a country that, scratch the surface, is as real as anywhere else. Scotland is complicated, richly so, and nowhere more obviously than in the labyrinthine world of Scotch whisky.

## FROM UNWRITTEN BEGINNINGS

The story of Scotch whisky begins in happy confusion. The very first mention of whisky being made in Scotland is as late as 1494, when Brother John Cor is recorded by the Exchequer Rolls as having taken receipt of 'eight bolls of malt to make aqua vitae'.

It's a tantalising piece of first evidence. Enough to be considered more than a kitchen and kettle operation, Friar John's order suggests a sizeably developed practice, no doubt one that had been going on for years, and on which it's highly unlikely he exercised a monopoly. As for whether knowledge of distilling beer had escaped the monastery and court, we can't say for sure. Certainly, Hector Boece's *The History and Chronicles of Scotland*, published in 1527, makes claims for a generations-old practice, while perhaps more factually revealing is an act in

1579 restricting distilling to earls, lords and barons that speaks volumes: people were making their own hooch, and enough of it to have become a threat.

Whatever the truth of its origins and early reach, Scotland's relationship with Boece's 'kind of aqua vitae' ('uisge beatha', a flavoured distillate) was such that, by the 1700s, 'consumption', writes Dave Broom, had 'become ritualised: it is sacrament, payment, the cornerstone of hospitality'.

## A FINE MESS

Tax records indicate that large-scale commercial distilleries were in operation in Scotland from at least the 1600s, the largest being the Ferintosh distillery, though it was during the eighteenth century that things really took off, with Lowland distilleries producing spirit for export to London, for the express purpose of being made into gin. This was a boom time for Lowland whisky makers.

Not forever, though – and never for everybody. A government-initiated stranglehold gradually took shape: a tax on capacity was introduced, forcing Lowland distillers to develop saucer-like stills capable of holding only small amounts of beer, and which discharged at breakneck speed, the result a high volume, very low-quality spirit. Gin makers in London lobbied successfully for a greater duty to be paid on Scottish exports. Home distilling was finally banned. Corruption was rife. Operations north of the Highland Line, largely farmer distiller size, were taxed into the ground, export south of the Highland Line outlawed.

By the turn of the nineteenth century many a maker had either gone to the wall or operated illegally. Highland whiskies had gained an increasingly better – though heavy and uneven – reputation, while Lowland whisky was an unmitigated disaster. Anyone who drank decent whisky drank 'Irish'. Scotch was what you drank in the shebeen, the tavern, or 'when in Scotland', a reputation it found difficult to shrug off, even after a fundamental relaxing of the law in 1823. Irish was made and consumed in Scotland. It was clearly – in the minds of many, the Scots included – the better stuff. Scotch was, on the other hand, as Broom says, 'a northern oddity'.

## DAY OF THE BLEND

If in any doubt as to the design element of revolutions, look no further than the evidence amassed by the Royal Commission on Whisky in 1908. The birth of the blend was in direct response to the Irish question: how to achieve the same uniformity of style as that of Irish whisky?

The answer, to the chagrin of purists, was to blend a small portion of grain whisky(s) with a number of single malts. Blending of just malts had been allowed under bond from 1853.

Private experiments with grain had been going on for years. The Spirit Act (1860) would bring everything together, legalising the blending of malt with grain whisky, the first official example of which was Scotch Ushers Old Vatted Glenlivet. The floodgates gaping, in came Johnnie Walker, Buchanans, John Dewar & Son, Greenlees Bros, Mackie & Co. All would eventually set up office in London, and from there expand into the Empire, their whiskies designed, as Samuel Greenlees would later report to the Commission, 'to suit the public at the time'.

Innovative, adaptable and highly competitive, the new Scottish whisky company was also a master of the idea of the brand, and spent as much time on consistency of image as it did product. It was utterly relentless in its pursuit of the market, managing during Prohibition to hobble the Irish, and so position itself to take full advantage of the years that followed. Fast forward to 1945 and the northern oddity was the meaning of top shelf whisky. Scotch had come an awful long way in an awful short time.

# GUIDE TO THE LABYRINTH

Today, Scotland has 109 active malt distilleries, located in one of six whisky making regions: Campbeltown, Lowlands, Speyside, Islay, Highlands and Islands, the last of which is legally classified as part of the Highlands, but in reality is treated by everybody as a separate entity. Of the current 109 distilleries, just seven are grain distilleries.

The Highlands and Speyside cover off every mainland distillery north of the old Highland Line, which runs at an angle from west of Glasgow to Dundee. The Highlands consists of 32 distilleries, from Glengoyne in the south to Old Pulteney in the north. North-eastern Speyside is a rough inverted triangle narrowing as it runs upriver either side of the Spey. It's home to 48 malt distilleries, most of which sit cheek-by-jowl, the most concentrated collection of distilleries in the world.

Major victim of a late nineteenth century blip, courtesy of Pattison, Elder & Co., whose flamboyant owners, the brothers Walter and Robert Pattison, floated a company neither worth the valuation nor wholly honest about the contents of its blends, the Lowlands is every mainland distillery (a comparably paltry 11) south of the Highland Line, except the three in Campbeltown, which, owing to its individual historical importance, retains status as a separate region. Similarly, Islay is on its own, and has eight distilleries. The rest of Scotland's islands make up the remaining seven distilleries, which stretch from Jura in the south west to Highland Park and Scapa in the north east.

There is no single good reason as to why the regions should shape up as they do. History and/or geography may explain distilleries existing in certain places, but they fail to account for why two distilleries within spitting distance of each other should produce two very different styles of single malt whisky.

Islay apart, there is no such thing as a regional style. Each region is its own mix of difference, each distillery its own universe.

The Scottish whisky industry is no longer owned by its founding families – or even by the giant blending houses that ruled the roost at the turn of the twentieth century. Over half of its active distilleries are owned by either Diageo (British) or Pernod Ricard (French), with the remainder divided between a mix of mainland Europe, British, South African and Asian companies. Founding families make up a tiny minority of Scottish distillery owners, the Grants being the most prominent.

Blends account for over 90% of Scotch's export market. Single malts make up about a fifth of the Scottish market. Single grain whisky is a tiny category, but very much the most exciting new area. Much has been said of the current boom, the diversity and depth of the market, but the industry is worth about £3.95 billion, down on the previous year (2014), which in turn was down on the year before. This said, Scotch remains the whisky world's giant.

## RETURN OF THE MALT

While always beloved by aficionados, single malt as a drink in itself had been stripped of all individuality by the success of the world of blends. Until the 1960s, very few whisky producers promoted single malts in and of themselves. It was an old drink. It was too full of flavour. It had no sex appeal.

## RULES AND PLAYERS

—For scotch to be Scotch, it must be matured in Scotland in oak casks for a minimum of three years.

—There are five distinct categories of Scotch whisky: single malt, single grain, blended Scotch, blended malt and blended grain.

—A single malt is made from 100% malted barley in a single distillery. A 'single grain whisky' is made in a single distillery from a mash of one or more grains and a portion of malted barley.

—A 'blended Scotch' is a blend of one or more grain whiskies with one or more single malts. A 'blended malt' is a blend of two or more malts hailing from different distilleries. A 'blended grain' is the same as a 'blended malt', only referring to grains rather than malt.

Until, that is, whisky's catastrophic slump in the 1980s. The reasons for its fall are many, with a world oil crisis playing a decisive role, but the industry as a whole was caught napping – sunning itself beside a gargantuan and now difficult-to-sell lake of 1970s whisky. The market retracted. Vodka took off. Distilleries haemorrhaged. The only way out was mass rationalisation, an in-house euphemism for frenzied self-amputation. By 1986, a quarter of Scottish distilleries were closed, with many of the survivors working at reduced capacities. Things looked worse than bad.

Out of the ashes, however, a liquid phoenix: the big, deep flavours as exemplified by many of Scotland's single malts. In the 1970s, the likes of Glenfiddich, the Macallan and the Glenlivet had gone against the market, promoted their malts, and sparked a small and vociferously loyal support. In 1986, Diageo launched its Classic Malts of Scotland series, as represented by six of its distilleries, and the support became a cult. People took notice and spread the word.

There's more to the story, of course, but much of the attention paid to single malts arose from their ability to mark themselves apart from the herd – blends, white spirits, you name it. Interesting, slightly uncomfortable, possibly an acquired taste, their very attraction was in their tricky approachability. They were stallions, different, headstrong, full of character. They demanded a special understanding, an education that took in not just the product, but also the whys and wherefores of its creation – distilleries, production, wood. Suddenly, a tipping point: the second age of the big flavour was back – and with it, the whole of Scotch whisky.

## FINE EXAMPLES

The following are age statement single malt whiskies. Blended Scotch and blended malt whiskies can be found on pages 54–55. No-age statement whiskies can be found on pages 128–9.

**Ardbeg 10** (46%) *Ardbeg Distillery* (Glenmorangie Group, Islay). In many a book the peated 10-year-old.

**Balvenie Portwood 21 (**40%) *Balvenie Distillery* (William Grant & Sons, Speyside). Perfect example of the perfect finish.

**Benromach 10** (43%) *Benromach Distillery* (Gordon and Macphail, Speyside). Great 10-year-old – made slowly.

**Bowmore 15 Darkest** (43%) *Morrison Bowmore Distillery* (Suntory, Islay). Peated and more aromatic than many of its neighbours. Try the Tempest and the 17. All fantastic.

**Craigellachie 13** (46%) *Craigellachie Distillery* (Bacardi, Speyside). Once the province ot the independent bottler, one of three age staggered official releases. Excellent.

**Caola Ila 12** (43%) *Caola Ila Distillery* (Diageo, Islay). Lovely peated whisky.

**Clynelish 14** (46%) *Clynelish Distillery* (Diageo, Highlands). True highland classic.

**Glenfiddich 18** (40%) *Glenfiddich Distillery* (William Grant & Sons, Speyside). Fabulous and affordable.

**Hazelburn 10** (46%) *Springbank Distillery* (J & A Mitchell & Co., Campbeltown). Wonderful product from one of the most uniquely traditional distilleries in the world.

**Highland Park 21** (47.5%) *Highland Park Distillery* (Edrington Group, Islands). Many people's number 1 single malt. Highland Park is in a league of its very own. The 12's very good, and much kinder on the wallet.

**Lagavulin 16** (43%) *Lagavulin Distillery* (Diageo, Islay). One of the absolute greats when it comes to peated whiskies.

**Laphroaig 10** (40%) *Laphroaig Distillery* (Beam Suntory, Islay). All power to the iodine. Great and affordable.

**Oban 14** (43%) *Oban Distillery* (Diageo, Highlands). Under the radar beauty.

**Old Pulteney 17** (46%) *Old Pulteney Distillery* (Inver House, Highlands). Another wonder.

**Talisker 18** (45.8%) *Talisker Distillery* (Diageo, Islands). The 10's good. This is excellent.

**The Laddie 10** (46%) *Bruichladdich Distillery* (Remy Martin, Islay). This is something to sit with. Ponder away.

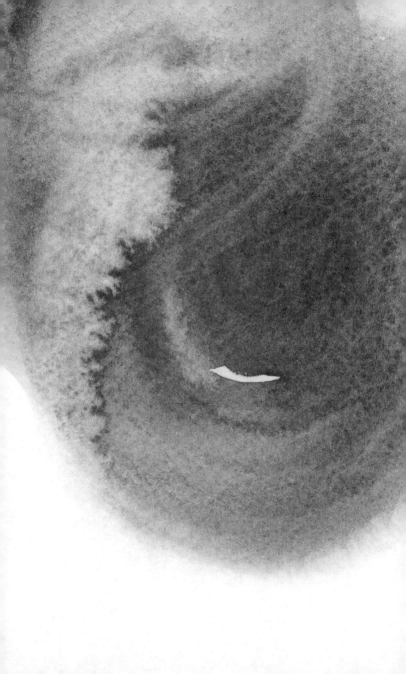

# 6

## AMERICA:
## BOURBON REBORN

Twenty years ago, the American whisky industry was at exactly rock bottom, the endpoint of a tailspin that began in the late 1970s. A new generation of drinkers had moved on, rye was an artefact and bourbon making, says Chris Morris, master distiller at Woodford Reserve, was 'on autopilot'. Now, of course, all has changed. It's the world's brown spirits darling. It's quite a story.

## AMERICA'S OWN

The very earliest American alcohol drinkers drank beer, cider, distilled cider (applejack) and rum – probably in that order. He or she also drank largely unaged whisky, though it would have been made from rye rather than barley or corn. Rye liquor took off when faltering molasses trade lines put paid to any rum making, in the main in Pennsylvania, where multi-generations of Europeans had already taken root.

However, America's own isn't rye. It's bourbon, a whisky made from maize (corn), a crop native to the Americas, and which grew well and fast in the frontier colonies, particularly in the likes of what was then the Kentucky District of Virginia, a land of rolling hills, and fed by countless waterways – perfect whisky-making country. Of all America's straight whiskies, bourbon is by far its most popular, followed by Tennessee whisky, which is also, as said (*see* page 14), technically a bourbon.

A number of today's bourbon brands argue the toss over

who the first bourbon distiller might be – Elijah Craig, Evan Williams – but no one really knows. Equally, no one's sure exactly how bourbon got its name. There are a number of theories, the strongest being that the Old Bourbon Whiskey stamped on casks shipped south referred to their source, Bourbon County, nicknamed Old Bourbon. That or bourbon historian Mike Veach's positing that a post-Independence pair of royalist-minded French entrepreneurs might have lifted it from one of the new whisky's destinations – Bourbon Street, New Orleans. Again, we're speculating.

## A LOST WAY

Owing to the peculiarities of its history, to the fact of National Prohibition and its wiping out of four-fifths of what was then a wonderfully heterogeneous collection of thousands of distilleries, the bourbon industry today is largely consolidated under the roofs of just a handful of producers, most of which are located in Kentucky or Tennessee: they are Wild Turkey, Heaven Hill, George Dickel, Four Roses, Brown-Forman, Beam Suntory, Sazarac, and the one interloper, MGP Indiana.

These are the survivors of bourbon's lost years, in one form or another. Following Prohibition and the Second World War, the habits and tastes of more than a generation of whisky drinkers had changed: scotch ruled the top shelf, Canadian

# AMERICAN STRAIGHT WHISKY: TERMS

—American straight whisky must be distilled at 80% abv or below, barrelled at no more than 62.5% abv, and aged in a new, charred oak barrel for at least two years. As well as bourbon, rye and corn, other straight whiskies include wheat, malt and a number of rarer and more exotic grains. All must be made from a mash of at least 51% of their title grain.

—If aged for below two years it is still, by definition, a whisky, but can't be called a straight whisky. If aged for below four years, it must carry an age statement. Colouring or flavours are not allowed, though a producer can release a straight whisky with added flavouring as long as it is labelled as such.

—As well as being defined as a whisky, for bourbon to be bourbon, it must be made in America from a mash of at least 51% corn. In reality, most bourbons are made from mashbills consisting of 70–76% corn, the rest being the small grain and a tiny amount of malted barley. A bourbon carrying a high percentage of rye is normally called a 'high rye', and any carrying wheat is a 'wheated bourbon'.

—While unusual, a bourbon can carry no small grain, which would usually qualify it as being a straight corn whisky – except that a corn whisky is the exception that proves the rule: it does not have to be aged to be called a whisky, and if it is, then it must be in a non-charred cask.

had stolen a march, producers were talking up blends and bourbon was perceived, says whisky writer Chuck Cowdery, as a 'workingman's drink'. It wasn't that it was bad. On the contrary, as any old bourbon bottle fan will tell you, some of it was very good. It was just that, with one or two notable exceptions, it wasn't sold as good – or great, or even properly.

Thus, whatever the extent of its recovery towards the middle of the twentieth century, bourbon in the 1980s was, in Morris's memorable phrase, on autopilot. The bourbon lake (whisky in bond) was a veritable and growing sea; young Americans had moved onto white spirits – and bourbon didn't know what to do. An industry bloodbath followed, ending in 1992 with the final closure of the Stitzel-Weller Distillery, very possibly Kentucky's greatest distillery.

## ON THE ROAD TO DIVERSITY

There are lots of reasons why bourbon has recovered, the most prosaic being that it had to – either that or disappear entirely. In other words, the generation-long tailspin was necessary: American whisky as a whole had to bottom out before anything else. It had to hit the bottom, look up and see a way back through all that vodka and white rum. That happened in 1994. As Cowdery says: 'At that point, the bourbon segment could start to compete for incremental share gains and slowly rebuild volume and profitability.'

At the same time, however, one or two distilleries and distillers had for years been ploughing their own particular furrows – Makers Mark (Beam Suntory), Four Roses and what was at the time the George T Stagg Distillery (now Buffalo Trace, Sazarac). Whether a whole production approach or simply an experimental line, these whisky makers were exploring notions of quality in the normal sense, but also as difference and as aspiration, efforts that did not go unnoticed. And nor did the cults they fostered – Makers in America, Four Roses and Stagg's Blanton Single Barrel abroad.

Taking a leaf out of the Scottish revival book, which had similarly rediscovered the allure of its own big, different, individual and strong whiskies, producers began to experiment with the idea of the premium. Out went the lighter tastes and in came a bolder, richer approach, a range of differentials, including higher strength bottlings, different strengths for the same expression each year, and single barrel and small batch offerings. Like single malts, these whiskies pointed the way to tickling the fancy of a new type of consumer. The big, fat, mouth-chewing bourbon was back, as was the beginning of a proper look at where, perhaps, production had lost its way.

And if these, the big producers, were beginning to reshape their own portfolios, their various successes tied to the noise of the premium, so outside of them has sprung a veritable revolution in small-scale whisky making (*see* pages 110–117). The American craft movement comprises literally hundreds of distilleries, situated throughout the country, their products an eclectic mix of the experimental and the rediscovery of lost and foreign traditions. As well as bourbon, rye's a favourite, and owes them its second coming, though pure corn's popular, as are wheat, malt and a range of more exotic grains.

In short, bourbon's back – and with it, the rest of American straight whisky. Kentucky bourbon has grown 150% since 2000. Tennessee's Jack Daniels is the world's most recognisable brand. Once dead in the water, rye has made an astonishing comeback – it being one of the industry's fastest growing categories. New distilleries, independent bottlers and brands are being born so fast it's almost impossible to keep track. Innovation and diversity's the name of the game. Asia's the mantra. Everyone's crossing their fingers.

## FINE EXAMPLES

Please note that whiskies made by craft distilleries are listed on pages 116–117.

**Blanton's Original Single Barrel** (103 proof/51.5%) *Buffalo Trace Distillery* (Sazarac). The single barrel that officially started it all.

**Booker's** (bottled at varying proofs) *Jim Beam Distillery* (Beam Suntory). A classic slap-and-stare-you-down small batch bourbon.

**Bulleit Bourbon** (90 proof /45%) *Distillery not divulged* (Diageo). Good example of a high rye bourbon – as is the slightly weaker version. Try the Bulleit Rye too.

**Colonel EH Taylor Small Batch** (100 proof/50%) *Buffalo Trace Distillery* (Sazarac) Not always easy to get, but a first-class bourbon, and reasonably priced considering.

**Four Roses Single Barrel** (100 proof/50%) *Four Roses Distillery* (Kirin). For the absolute beginner and for the absolute connoisseur. A Buddha of bourbons.

**George T Stagg** (varying bottling proof, though known to hit a staggering 142 proof/71%) *Buffalo Trace Distillery* (Sazarac). One to be tried in army fatigues.

**Johnny Drum Private Stock** (101 proof/50.5%) *Distillery not divulged.* Broker and bottler: *Kentucky Bourbon Distillers* (KBD). Excellent bang-for-your-buck whisky.

**Noah's Mill** (114.3 proof/57.15%) *Distillery not divulged.* Broker and bottler: *Kentucky Bourbon Distillers* (KBD). Huge, experimental, ballsy. After this, try Rowan's Creek – also KBD.

**Old Forester Birthday Bourbon** (proof varies) *Early Times Distillery* (Brown Forman). Though not the easiest to find, and changes from year to year, an excellent value bourbon.

**Rittenhouse Straight Rye** (100 proof/50%) *Heaven Hill Bernheim Distillery* (Heaven Hill). Really good rye. If you're willing to spend, and can find it, then try the 25-year-old.

**Sazarac 18** (90 proof/45%) *Buffalo Trace Distillery* (Sazarac). One of the best straight ryes ever. The younger, higher strength Thomas H Handy is equally fine.

**Wild Turkey 101** (101 proof/52%) *Wild Turkey Distillery* (Bacardi). Massive mouth-filler. Perfect example of why low-strength barrel fills get so much more from the wood.

**W L Weller 12** (90 proof/45%) *Buffalo Trace Distillery* (Sazarac). For many, the demi-god of wheated bourbons.

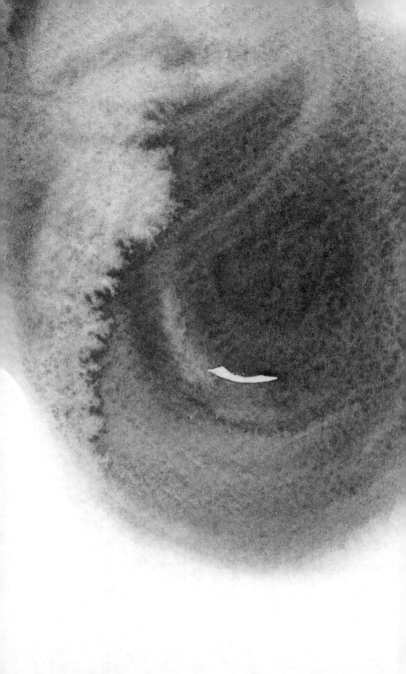

# 7 JAPAN: THE POST-PERFECT OF COPY

The late Octavio Paz, poet, author and Mexico's most ardent champion of the surreal, once claimed that copying is the beginning of creativity. I am paraphrasing here, but it's a wonderfully simple proposition: when it comes to writing a poem, painting a picture or, indeed, making a style of whisky, it is impossible to duplicate that which has come before. Make a copy and you instantly create.

Nothing, in this respect, could be truer of Japanese whisky making, which in less than a hundred years has taken a Scottish form and turned it into a style that, while paying due homage to its precursor, melds science to that of a design sensibility that presents depth with the very lightest of touches. A Japanese distiller making whisky in Japan could not hope to make anything but a Japanese whisky, such is the influence of tradition, climate, need and desire.

Thus is it that, in 2014, Suntory's Yamazaki Sherry Cask won Jim Murray's Whisky Bible's world's best whisky title. It's a malt. It's made in the Scottish tradition, with Scottish malted barley. But it's not Scottish. It's Japanese. It's a Japanese malt whisky, and one so influential that, like many a Japanese whisky, it informs how we read, understand and taste Scottish whiskies. The supposed copy precedes its template; the successor, its precursor. Paz the surrealist would be delighted.

# A POEM OF A WHISKY STORY

Japan's love affair with whisky begins with the story of an American captain, his ship and the gift of a cask – delivered in 1854, to the feet of a living god. Whisky, one supposes, did what whisky does best: the Emperor gave holy assent, Japan opened its gates, and scotch was in.

In fact, when Commodore Matthew C Perry made good his promise to force it into trade, Japan was yet to replace the ruling shogun with the young and more western-friendly Emperor Meiji, then more figurehead than holy appointee.

It would take another 14 years and an insurrection before the west got its way. In the meantime, the odds on Perry's liquid softener – bourbon or scotch, no one's sure – making it intact, from ship to god, were slim to none. To be clear, the whisky was (probably) nicked.

Nonetheless, Perry did succeed. The Tokugawa Shogunate did acquiesce. As it happens, torn apart by civil war, America was unable to capitalise on its early success, and so Britain – and therefore scotch – was able to fill the breach, forging a special relationship that saw Scottish whisky, unobtainable and therefore extraordinary, become a Japanese status symbol, a rare and special gift, a drink that was easily assimilated into its age-old drinking cultures.

Taxed to the hilt, its relative scarcity birthed a whole industry of spirits rectifiers, all cashing in on the new westernised taste, and it is out of this early milieu that Japan was able to set about forging its own whisky-making tradition.

## BIRTH OF A NEW TRADITION

While there is some evidence to suggest the influence of much lesser known contemporaries, Japanese whisky owes its success to a history set in motion by the dreams of two men: a young chemist, Masataka Taketsuru, and Shinjiro Torii, both of whom wanted to make whisky themselves – their own Japanese whisky.

Briefly, in 1919, Taketsuru was sent by his firm to Scotland in order to learn the trade and so return and begin to make whisky in its name. Married, his Scottish bride, Rita, in tow, Taketsuru returned to find his employer had given up on starting a whisky distillery. He was subsequently hired by Torii, and in 1923 helped found Japan's first whisky distillery, now Suntory's Yamazaki. Distillation began in 1924 and the rest, as they say, is history, though it's not quite as neat a story as you might think, the pair parting over their first creation: Shirofuda.

The details as to exactly how are shrouded in good manners, but the why of it is perfectly clear. Torii was after a lighter, more subtly peated whisky, Taketsuru a heavyweight. The market sided with Torii: Shirofuda was, as he had predicted, way too rich for the Japanese palate. It bombed. Taketsuru looks to have been sidelined, and left the company when he could. He would go on to found a juice and cider company, which morphed into producing apple brandy – before settling into whisky production at Yoichi, still Japan's most northern distillery. Taketsuru's new company was eventually renamed Nikka.

## A PAIR OF GIANTS

Today, Suntory and Nikka have two major distilleries apiece (Yamazaki and Hakushu, Yoichi and Miyagikyo), as well as Chita (Suntory) and Tochigi (Nikka), their dedicated grain distilleries. The first and also biggest of Japan's whisky makers, they produce the vast majority of Japanese whisky. It's a remarkable story, though nothing like plain sailing, especially in the beginning. However, if things got off to a relatively slow start for both, then the war brought growing custom, as did Japan's economic miracle, while a vibrant and ever-changing bar culture has periodically helped push things on and through the inevitable generational backlash.

At the same time, the competition has not fared nearly as well, with a number of eminent distilleries falling foul of Japan's 1990s economic meltdown. International attention and the upturn in all matters whisky means things are much better now, and the number of distilleries is, once again, on the rise.

Old or new, they are Fuji-Gotemba, Shinshu, Chichibu and Eigashima, though it's going to be years before all but Gotemba will be able to compete in terms of age and volume of stock. Prized whiskies from closed or dismantled distilleries include Karuizawa and Hanyu. The latter is a fine example of a distillery closed partially on account of its whisky being thought of as not good, only to discover that it ages beautifully.

## A WHISKY DESIGNED

While different both in themselves and from the rest of the competition, Suntory's Yamazaki and Hakushu distilleries serve, in their own ways, as perfect examples of what makes Japanese whisky of its own.

In keeping with an ethos that emphasises the new as much as it does the old, each has happily de-rigged and rebuilt itself, and more than once – this in an industry that, according to urban lore, insists on replacing a knackered still with its exact replica, dents and all. Considering the significance of distillery character, on the new make, and therefore on the final product, the willingness to tear down the old and start afresh speaks volumes. For Suntory, risking the new is an integral part of what it means to make very good whisky.

And through all this, so runs a tradition of absolute self-sufficiency. Unlike their Scottish counterparts, Japanese producers do not trade whiskies for blending purposes. Meaning, if trading with each other is not an option, and buying in from abroad is unsustainable, then the only answer is to make it yourself. To wit, both Yamazaki and Hakushu use multiple levels of peated and unpeated barley, multiple yeasts, multiple stills, multiple new makes, multiple wood types, multiple casks, the sum being vast theatres of whisky-making variables, the outcomes of which would test a computer, and yet neither crumples under the weight of the thought that goes into its making. On the contrary, their whiskies emerge considered, and beautiful, and utterly unique – and there are lots of them.

Together, Suntory and Nikka are in a league of two when it comes to options, but the competition, whether mothballed or today's current crop, are renowned for whiskies equally fine, equally sought after. The world's best blended malt at the 2013 International Spirits Challenge went not to Suntory or Nikka, but rather to Shinshu's economically entitled Mars Maltage 3 + 25. Chichibu Distillery, meanwhile, new and beautifully thought through, is putting out young whiskies that promise real greatness. There are other horses in this race, and provided the market holds, there may be more to come. The world can barely wait.

# FINE EXAMPLES

The following include malts and blends. In the event that a blend is taken from more than one distillery, the master blender responsible is named in place of a single distillery.

**Chichibu Peated** (53%) *Chichibu Distillery*. Good example of how attention to detail makes a young-in-years whisky taste and feel utterly mature.

**Coffey Grain Whisky** (45%) *Miyagikyo Distillery* (Nikka). Mainly corn and distilled in a column still. Sounds – but doesn't taste – American. Light and highly perfumed.

**Hakushu 12** (43%) *Hakushu Distillery* (Suntory). Peaty, deep, affordable. If money's no object, try the 18.

**Hibiki 21** (43%) *Seiichi Koshimizu (retired)/Shinji Fukuyo (present)* (Suntory). A blend of malts from both of Suntory's big distilleries. World class.

**Karuizawa 1981–1984** (varying cask strengths) *Karuizawa Distillery* (closed – now exclusively bottled by No 1 Drinks Company). Mainly sherry casks, but some bourbon. Hard to get, but great value consdering rarity.

**Mars Malt: The Revival** (58%) *Hombo Mars Distillery*.
Perfect example of a revived distillery (Hombo) making
whisky so good as to be released at extremely young ages.
This one is only three and is a belter.

**Nikka Coffey Malt Whisky** (45%) *Miyagikyo Distillery*
(Nikka). Cracking column distilled malt. Breaks all the rules.

**Nikka Whisky From The Barrel** (51.4%) *Tadashi Sakuma*
(Nikka). Blend from all three of Nikka's distilleries. One to
turn a dyed-in-the-wool malt head.

**Taketsuru 17** (43%) *Miyagikyo Distillery* (Nikka).
A masterclass in the art of Japanese (malt) blending.

**The Nikka 12** (43%) *Tadashi Sakuma* (Nikka). A new and
brilliantly blended whisky. Excellent value.

**Yamazaki 18** (43%) *Yamazaki Distillery* (Suntory).
Everything we've said, in one bottle. One of the world's best
single malts.

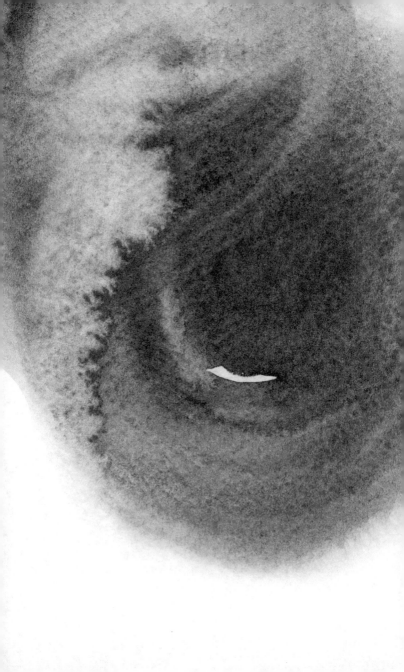

# 8

## IRELAND: A NEW MOON

When asked what piece of advice he might pass onto the next generation of Irish entrepreneurs, John Teeling, founder of Ireland's Cooley and Teeling distilleries, once said: 'When you get ten rejections, get another ten.'

He may have been referring to the world of business in general, but Teeling's words serve as fair strap-line for the sheer tenacity of Irish whisky itself. It's riding high now, but in 1987, when he set up Cooley, whisky making in Ireland had reached such a low as to be represented by a grand total of just two distilleries: Bushmills in Northern Ireland and Midleton in County Cork. Rejection's not the word. This was Irish whisky almost dead. Or so it seemed.

At any rate, contrary to what is generally thought of as being Irish whisky – that is, triple distilled, a predominant style, and a range of blends – is actually only a part of a much bigger picture. Ireland is home to three of the four whisky styles, as much to single malt and grain whiskies as it is Irish pot still, to most types of still and methods of distillation, and so to a variety of whisky that, while unable to match Scotland for number, offers real choice. It's small, but it's a veritable pantheon.

# TOP OF THE PILE

In a world obsessed with firsts, the debate as to who in the British Isles first distilled beer – the Irish, the Scots, perhaps, even, an Anglo-Saxon – masks the extent of Ireland's contribution to fine whisky making. What matters is not so much the order in which everyone got out of those early blocks, but rather how things developed once up and running.

In this respect, Irish whisky by the late 1500s was already recognised as something special. Usquebaugh, a redistilled and flavoured new make, was consumed, as Dave Broom notes, alongside 'uisege breathahd' (aqua vitae or straight new make), and seems to have earned special recognition as an Irish 'usque', a style of whisky like no other. 'A sovereign liquid', said Raphael Holinshed, author of *The Chronicles of England, Scotland and Ireland* (1577), relatively tasty and capable of the extraordinary, 'it slows age, it strengthens youth, it helps digestion, it cuts phlegm, it abandons melancholy, it relieves the heart, it lightens the mind, it quickens the spirit'.

Usquebaugh: a godly pick-me-up. By 1755 it had so cemented its reputation for consistency of quality as to move Samuel Johnson to describe it as being not only 'particularly distinguished by its pleasant and mild flavour', but also as palpably different from the 'Highland sort' (Scottish), which was 'somewhat hotter'. Irish whisky was whisky.

## TRIPLE DISTILLED

Whatever Johnson was drinking in the mid-1700s, things had changed up a number of gears by the turn of the nineteenth century. Having survived a raft of relatively punitive taxes, with many a distillery opting to go dark, Irish whisky was well placed to make the most of a relaxing of regulations when they came (1823), especially in terms of developing consistency of flavour.

The early 1800s witnessed the birth of a method of double distillation that saw the low wines divided into weak and strong, redistilled separately, the feints from both reserved for the next batch of weak low wines, the rest distilled as spirits, the result a stronger and cleaner final distillate. A halfway house, it's a method that served as bridge between double and triple distillation, largely giving way to the latter in the late 1800s, which in combination with a later trend for very large pots served to reinforce Irish whisky's standing for a consistently refined and elegant whisky.

In addition, as is so often the way, necessity provided creativity further impetus, the nineteenth century malt tax resulting in increasing numbers of distillers adding portions of unmalted barley to the mash, the outcome a slightly more acidic, oily, peppery fruity taste to the new make, and with it, the birth of a new style: Irish pot still whisky.

Cashing in on its reputation, Irish whisky began for the first time to properly exploit Ireland's position in the union, and as a result grew exponentially, with Dublin housing a clutch – Jameson (John), Roe, Power and Jameson (William) – of the world's largest distilleries, and Belfast and Cork contributing their fair share in terms of volume. Triple distilled, pot still, peated or unpeated, it's the 1860s and Irish whisky's the toast of the whisky-drinking world.

## FROM KING TO COFFEE

Nothing lasts, of course – and especially not empires. When it came, Irish whisky's fall from grace was swift, the result, as Broom says, of 'the cruellest run of bad luck, bad management and government interference'.

Briefly, the Dublin quartet's refusal to accept blended – 'silent' or 'sham' – whisky had long sown the seeds of Irish whisky's downfall. It's wrong, as often assumed, to suppose that the Irish whisky industry as a whole was against the use of column or continuous stills, which produced grain whiskies largely for the purpose of blends. There were Coffey stills in Belfast. There was a Coffey still at Midleton. Ireland was not just about the pot. No doubt the Dubliners believed wholly in their 'real whisky', but there was in their seemingly backward-looking fight an element of economic sense: the column was a threat to what until then had been the largest whisky production unit in the world. Not only was there going to be a new type of whisky, but the continuous still served notice on the age of the giant pot still.

Truth be known, the Dublin faction was too strong for its own good, and way behind the times. The increasing success of nineteenth century Scottish blenders was a direct reflection of a sea-change in the whisky drinking world's taste buds. Having backed themselves into a very conservative corner, things went from bad to worse – for the traditionalists and for Irish as a whole. Blended whisky was recognised in law (1909). The First World War happened. The Irish War of Independence (1919–1921) and Prohibition (1920–1933) deadheaded Ireland's main whisky markets. Distilleries were sold off, one after the other. Another world war later and Irish whisky was on its knees. The Scots had cleaned up, exercising a ruthless buy-to-kill policy, shutting down whatever they bought. The world wanted blends, and it was going to be scotch. A new king was born.

And the Irish were left out for the crows. In 1966 there were only four Irish distilleries in production, their annual output a smidgen against the 108 million odd litres produced at the turn of the century. An urban myth has it that but for the invention of a whisky coffee in Foynes, Western Ireland, popularised by the Buena Vista Hotel in San Francisco, it might have died out entirely. True or not, the industry was forced to rationalise, and ruthlessly. All but Bushmills was brought under a single roof, at Midleton, in Cork, the remaining traces of an empire

# IRISH WHISKY TERMS

—The Irish Whisky Act of 1980 defines Irish whisky as being made from a mash of cereal(s), fermented and then distilled at or at less than 94.8% abv, after which it must be aged for a minimum of three years in wooden casks.

—While Irish labelling employs similar terminology to Scotch whisky, the law doesn't go as far as to statutorily define what's meant, for example, by 'single pot still' or 'single malt' whisky. As in Scotland, 'single' denotes a whisky as coming from a single distillery. 'Pot still', meanwhile, refers to whisky made from a mash containing both unmalted and malted barley. Malt we know.

—Traditionally, Irish pot still whisky is triple distilled, though there's no law to say it should be. Not all Irish whisky is triple distilled.

—If made from a blend of two distillates, then an Irish whisky must be labelled as 'blended'. A blended Irish whisky will come from either trade between two or more distilleries or from two or more different distillates – grain, malt or pot still – made at the same distillery. Usually, the 'blend' is a portion of grain and pot still or malt whiskies.

—To be considered 'Irish', a whisky needs to have been distilled and aged in the 'State or in Northern Ireland'.

now in the hands of Irish Distillers Ltd (IDL), a monopoly dedicated to keeping a score of brands alive.

## FROM ASHES

In light of the speed and depth of its fall, Irish whisky's recovery is often described as something of a miracle. And indeed, in many ways, it is. Hitching a ride on the back of the general whisky recovery, and in particular the re-emergence of a taste for single malt and bourbon, the category has gone ballistic.

However, as with most miracles, someone clever's had a hand in the wonder. IDL planned ahead. It initiated the world's first wood policy. It pulled down the Midleton distillery in 1975, and built a new and much more adaptable one. It held its nerve, so much so that by the time Teeling entered the fray, the results of its changes were already out, and beginning to attract critical acclaim. Irish was on its way back.

It wasn't an easy ride, though. Cooley nearly went down, saved in the end by an advance from Heaven Hill, who agreed to buy up stock early. The old foe, scotch, was riding strong, and so too, more recently, bourbon. Plus, as an industry, it's nothing like the size it was. It's narrow, with stock largely concentrated in the hands of just three distilleries. Even so, the emphasis on quality, on points of Irish difference, paid off – handsomely. Irish whisky's potential was enough to attract deep pockets.

IDL sold up: Midleton went to Pernod Ricard; Bushmills went to Diageo and is now Jose Cuervo. Teeling eventually sold to Beam – now Beam Suntory.

Giants aside, the distillery count's been ticking up – Teeling (now Jack, son of John), West Cork, the Echlinville, Tullamore, Kilbeggan, the Alltech Craft Distillery and Dingle. Old brands revived, new ones invented. Pot stills, columns, peated malts, different types of distillations, blends, grains – you name it, it's happening in Ireland.

Written off by the competition, defying all doomsayers, Irish whisky just would not, to reappropriate Teeling, lie down. On the contrary: it's a rocket, and provided the taxman lays off – and the market stays true, and the obsession with pushing Jamesons isn't at the expense of all else – then the moon's as Irish as it gets.

## FINE EXAMPLES

**Bushmills Black Bush** (40%) *Bushmills Distillery* (Jose Cuervo). For some, the Irish blend.

**Bushmills Malt 10** (40%) *Bushmills Distillery* (Jose Cuervo). Wonderful malt. Try the 16 for extra mixed wood action.

**Connemara 12 Peated** (40%) *Cooley Distillery* (Beam Suntory). Double distilled and peated. A great Irish single malt.

**Greenore 8** (40%) *Cooley Distillery* (Beam Suntory). Fine grain.

**Green Spot** (40%) *New Midleton Distillery* (Pernod Ricard). Single pot still and cult classic. Produced exclusively for brokers Mitchell's of Dublin.

**Jameson Special Reserve 12** (40%) *New Midleton Distillery* (Pernod Ricard). A blend among blends.

**Kilbeggan 15** (40%) *Old Kilbeggan Distillery* (Beam Suntory). At the moment a mix of Cooley matured on site. Great and affordable blend.

**Midleton Very Rare** (40%) *New Midleton Distillery* (Pernod Ricard). A highly sophisticated blend.

**Powers Gold Label** (40%) *New Midleton Distillery* (Pernod Ricard). Fine example of an Irish blend – pot still and a sniff of grain.

**Redbreast 12** (46%) *New Midleton Distillery* (Pernod Ricard). Single pot still and a giant to boot. The cask strength's a proper boss. The 21's where you're going on payday.

**Teeling Single Grain** (46%) *Teeling Irish Whiskey Company*. Juice sourced from Cooley. Wine cask matured. Great, young, fruity grain whisky.

**Teeling Single Malt** (46%) *Teeling Irish Whiskey Company*. More Cooley whisky put to splendid use.

**Tyrconnell Sherry Cask** (46%) *Cooley Distillery* (Beam Suntory). Single malt. An old brand revived.

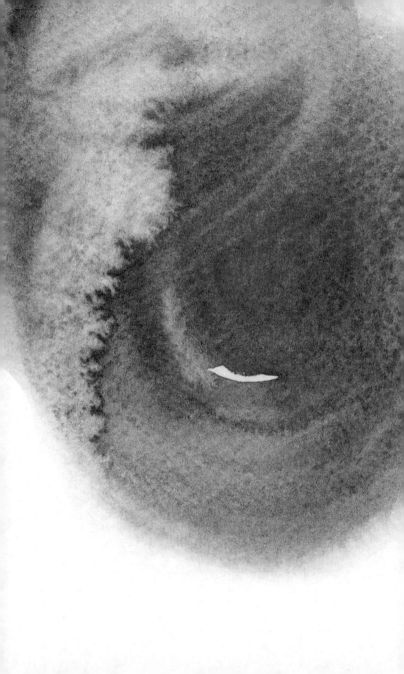

# 9

## CANADA: BIG IS BEAUTIFUL

When the sixteenth century French navigator and explorer Jacques Cartier, in his hunt for a passage to China, first laid eyes on 'the country of the Canadas', his disappointment was palpable: 'I am inclined', he said, 'to believe this is the land God gave to Cain'.

Cartier never did find the way to China, and nor did he succeed in his secondary aim, the discovery of the fabled Kingdom of Saguenay, land of rubies, gold and diamonds. Rather, having claimed 'Asia' for France on his first trip, penetrated as far as the rock of Quebec on his second, and on the third established, after the Vikings, 'Kanata', a second European colony, Cartier's legacy is to have mapped a 1000 mile stretch of the St Lawrence river. 'The world', he said, 'is big and still hides a lot'.

## THE SECRET BIG WORLD OF CANADIAN WHISKY

That Canada should seem to hide itself from Cartier will come as no surprise to anyone who knows anything about this vast and staggeringly beautiful country. Canada has always suffered the impression of being unknowable, and not least its whiskies, which 'like Canadians themselves', says whisky writer Davin de Kergommeaux, tend 'to fly under the radar'.

Truth is, Canadian whisky hides in plain sight, and in a big way. The most efficient method for the then largely English miller-settlers to recycle their grist, the nineteenth century saw a phenomenal growth in distilleries making 'common' (wheat) and barley whiskies, the most prominent of pioneers being Thomas Molson, who grew an enormous business off the back of exports to London.

And not just Molson. In its heyday the Molson Distillery in Montreal was huge, one of the world's largest, but what followed was something else: Gooderham and Worts, in Toronto, their mid-nineteenth century distillery a state-of-the-art facility capable of seven and a half million litres a year. Corbys in Hayden's Corners. Wisers in Prescott. Seagrams in Berlin, now Waterloo. Walkers in Windsor. Many prospered as a result of America's civil war, a select few during Prohibition, and Seagrams had a good go at taking over the twentieth century. All were giants.


## A WONDERFUL LIGHTNESS OF BEING

Seagrams' Sam Bronfman's much quoted shirt-sleeve-to-shirt-sleeve in three generations philosophy holds true not just for his own empire, but also for the majority of the aforementioned giants, sold off either by uninterested grandchildren or out of necessity, there being no one to take up the family reins – Corbys being an excellent example.

However, whatever the change of guard, Canadian

## WAY OF THE CANADIAN

Canadian whisky is a grain-based distillate that must be mashed, distilled, and aged (for at least three years) in Canada. Caramel colouring and flavouring is permitted. Extra defining criteria may apply depending on province of origin.

Present large-scale distilleries include Alberta, Black Velvet, Highwood, Gimli, Hiram Walker, Forty Creek, Valleyfield and Canadian Mist. This list is slightly complicated by the fact that different companies may own brands produced in distilleries owned by the competition. Glenora Distillery is smaller and Canada's first single malt distillery. A clutch of micro-distilleries have also just got off the ground. The vast majority of Canadian blended whiskies are single distillery whiskies.

Unlike their bourbon counterparts, Canadian whisky producers generally do not mix their grains before fermenting and distilling, preferring to distil and mature grains separately, and then blend the matured spirits to create the final whisky.

These matured spirits consist of the 'base' whisky and the 'flavouring' whisky. Normally corn, the base whisky comes off the stills at around 94% abv. The flavouring whisky – usually rye, but also wheat, corn or barley – comes off at much lower levels of alcohol content. The base whisky is matured in used casks, while the flavouring utilises either new or a mix of new and old casks.

Traditionally, the base whisky draws most of its flavour from the barrel and interactions within the barrel, which accounts for why a Canadian whisky is referred to as a rye, it being the most commonly used flavouring grain.

Variations on the above: Canadian Club and Black Velvet whiskies are made by blending the new make base spirit with newly made or partially matured flavouring spirit. A small but growing number of products are indeed 100% rye. The single malt productions at Glenora and Shelter Point are pot stilled as opposed to column.

whisky was a twentieth century success story. Prohibition America may not, as previously thought, have been awash with Canadian, with many a producer suffering the loss of its largest export market, but it certainly made the most of an American consumer turned onto lighter blends. As de Kergommeaux says, it played a significant role in the cocktail revolution, its subtlety of character perfectly attuned to the general shift in palate, the propensity of certain whiskies for 'leaping', as Dave Broom says, 'into life' once mixed.

Light, elegant and eminently consumable, Canadian whisky was a rocket between 1945 and 1980, outselling nearly all, and in particular bourbon, for which its corn-base sweetness was frequently mistaken.

## THE FALL AND THE RISING

As with the rest of the world, the 1980s saw Canadian whisky suffer the rise of white spirits, its count of 22 distilleries falling away to what has ended up as nine major distilleries.

Even so, while it may have been similarly affected, Canadian whisky's relative success prior to the rise of vodka has, until recently, had the effect of labelling the product as eternally light, its reputation for ease of sipping, for being good to mix with, giving the impression of being less than suited to a resurgent heavy duty palate. Thus, whatever the success of its sales, the last two decades saw it perceived by the noisy world of the whisky enthusiast as not possessing the sipping gumph of either single malt or bourbon whiskies.

Which is unfair – and not at all reflective of a market as enamoured by blends as it has always been. Truth is, Canadian whisky has long hidden its gems behind size as volume, and behind a specifically historical predilection for semi-anonymity – so much so that even Canadians are only really just beginning to access that which it offers by way of depth and quality. So, less Cain's lot, more a liquid Kingdom of Saguenay, Canadian whisky is full of wonder, and beginning to show it. Watch this space.

## FINE EXAMPLES

**Alberta Premium Dark Horse** (45%) *Alberta* (Beam Suntory). A 92% rye-grain whisky and fine example of Canada's recent super-premium output.

**Canadian Club Chairman's Select 100% Rye Whisky** (40%) *Alberta* (Beam Suntory). Exactly what it says on the tin.

**Caribou Crossing Single Barrel** (40%) *Sourced from any one of several distilleries* (Sazarac). The first Canadian single barrel expression since much vaunted Bush Pilot's.

**Crown Royal XO** (40%) *Gimli* (Diageo). Smoother than smooth can be. Proper example of Canadian single distillery blend.

**Crown Royal Hand Selected Barrel** (51.5%) *Gimli* (Diageo). Another single barrel bottling, this time of Coffey rye, traditionally used for blends. Not easy to get, but included as a perfect sign of things to come.

**Forty Creek John's Private Cask No 1** (40%) *Forty Creek Distillery* (Campari). The power of spice – and low strength too. Should lead you onto the Double Barrel and just about anything else with John Hall's name on it.

**Gibson's Finest Rare 18** (40%) *Valleyfield / Hiram Walker Distillery* (William Grant & Sons). One of the best Canadians money can buy. Now made at Walkers, though bottlings from stock matured at Valleyfield will be kicking around for years.

**Highwood Ninety 20** (45%) *Highwood Distillers* (Highwood). Another fine example of a Canadian base whisky.

**Lot 40** (43%) *Hiram Walker Distillery* (Pernod Ricard). Another all rye – old school in brand new clothes.

**Mastersons 10 Year Old Straight Rye** (45%) *Sourced from Alberta distillers* (35 Maple Street). Example of a Canadian bottled in America. Really great rye.

**Wiser's 18** (40%) *Hiram Walker Distillery* (Pernod Ricard). This is wood at its tobacco and Christmas pudding limits – and evidence that a 100% base whisky can pack a lot of power.

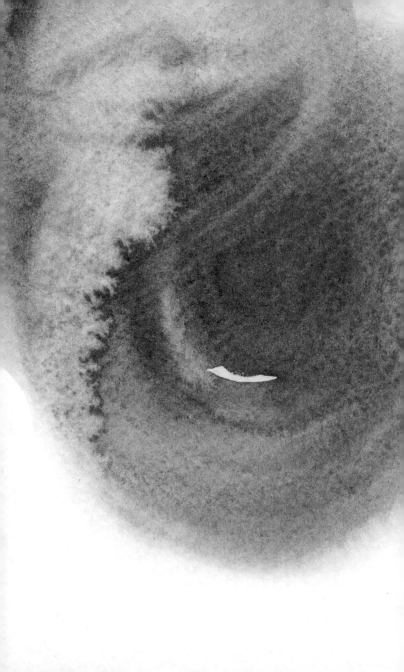

# 10 CRAFT AND OTHER WHISKY: A BRAVE NEW WORLD

In 2012 the unthinkable happened. A single malt whisky made in Waco, Texas won the prestigious Best in Glass Award. Dubbed the Judgement of London, craft distillery Balcones's Texas Single Malt defeat of Scotland and Japan's denizens was just the ticket: the brave new whisky world of the very small, the different and the other had finally arrived.

Which is a slightly dramatic way of saying that the last two or three years have seen some of the excesses of boomtown whisky come home to bite producers on much fattened behinds. While the actual volume of the last thirty years' worth of Scotch whisky sold isn't nearly what one might assume, there's no doubt that demand has resulted in a real quickening up of the whisky-making process, the choice of grain, the shortening of fermentation times, the ramping up of highly automated facilities, the faster distillations, all designed with one thing in mind: higher yield. Not everyone, of course, and not just Scotland, but enough for the old guard to suddenly seem much more about line graphs and numbers than they are tradition and innovation.

True or not, this general sense of some of the larger producers having lost touch with their roots has allowed for new-old ways of thinking about whisky making, the gaps left by the giants suddenly filled by an entirely new breed of maker, be that the likes of micro-distiller Corsair or the much larger set-up at Taiwan's Kavalan.

# THERE'S BEEN A REVOLUTION

At the turn of the century, America's whisky was made almost entirely by 13 distilleries, the infinitesimal remainder by a clutch of micro-distilleries. There are today over 500 distilleries in the US, a revolution built off both the back of the craft beer movement and the championing of alternative and traditional visions of consumption, such as the green and slow food movements.

America's where it's at, although to a lesser degree craft and small scale enterprises are springing up across the world, and nearly all share the wonderful precariousness that marks a revolution in the making. These distilleries are often loud, always passionate and are generally vulnerable to the very costliness of making whisky.

This strange mix of noise, brilliance and vulnerability couldn't be better exemplified by Balcones itself, which was founded by Chip Tate, but saw him lose a majority share to investors and eventually having to accept a buyout – this despite a slew of world class awards. A personal tragedy, but also predictable, if not in Tate's case, then certainly generally speaking.

However meaningful, craft and micro-still whisky distilleries are exceptionally exposed, given tight margins, low volumes and the length of time it takes to get a whisky to market.

## THE MEANING OF CRAFT, NEW WORLD AND OTHER REVOLUTIONARY TERMS

A craft distillery is defined by the American Distilling Institute (ADI) as being capable of an output of no more than 100,000 proof gallons. It should be 75% or more owned or controlled by industry members who are 'materially involved in the production'. In this respect, craft is a form of production that has at every stage, and every creation, the mark or hand of its creator. Lateral thinking, speed, surprise and living outside of the box are its calling cards.

While not necessarily labelling themselves as such, the many so-called new world distilleries are comparably small enterprises, and value the same working practices as their self-defined craft cousins. Together, they marry the forgotten to the new, champion locally sourced and exotic varietals of grain and yeast, the pot over pure column, detail over spirit-making pace, and insist on controlling every aspect of production. Quality over yield is their baseline modus operandi.

It would be wrong, however, to suppose all new world distilleries are either small or defined by a craft ethos. A good few are modelled on large Scottish productions, their capacity bigger than anything that might be considered craft, their facilities mechanised, their set-ups overwhelmingly industrial. Common to all, though, is the fact that they are new and largely located in parts of the world with no great tradition of whisky making. Borrowing from the old, and from a whole range of other traditions, be they spirit or wine production, they operate in a geography – physical and cultural – entirely of their own, one that is as different and unexplored as it is new.

Seen this way, and much like craft, new world whisky has the fantastically oxymoronic character of both respecting and reinventing tradition. It's a new useful art form. It pays its dues and it cocks a snook – sometimes in the same breath. As such, and as is always the way of the sudden and rapid spread of a form of making, the idea of what constitutes the drink whisky is on the super move – and we're very much better off for the fact that it is.

## A QUICK WORD

This being a brave new world, with certain distilleries approaching or passing capacity, and much needed investment bringing both relief and a fundamental loss of control, craft as a specifically defined entity continues to evolve. One of the fastest growing sectors in American whisky, it's clearly a mighty popular bandwagon, with less than welcome fellow travellers including producers who fail to disclose not making the distillate themselves and those for whom the word gargantuan was invented. The revolution continues.

## FINE EXAMPLES

Note, the below are a mix of craft and/or new world whiskies. It's impossible to do justice in this short space to what's out there, so consider this a starting point.

**Amrut Fusion** (50%) *Amrut Distillery* (Amrut, India). Cracking single malt whisky.

**Balcones Crooked Texas Straight Bourbon** (125.6 proof/62.8%) *Balcones Distillery* (Balcones Distilling, Texas). Corn is how they made their name. This came just after the single malt. Try the Brimstone for a smoked corn whisky.

**Belgian Owl Single Malt 4** (46%) *The Owl Distillery* (Belgian Owl, Belgium). Highly craft conscious, the Owl has put out a number of young, different aged single malts.

**Corsair Triple Smoke** (80 proof/40%) *Corsair Artisan Distillery* (Corsair Distillery, Tennessee). Craft in a bottle. Full of attitude, heavily innovative.

**Kavalan Single Malt** (40%) *Kavalan King Car Whisky Distillery* (King Car Corporation, Taiwan). Actually, try anything from this distillery. Absolute world beaters.

**Koval Single Barrel Bourbon** (94 proof/46%) *Koval Distillery* (Koval, Chicago). Organic and very clean.

**Mackmyra Brukswhisky** (41.4%) *Mackmyra Distillery* (Mackmyra Svensk Whisky, Sweden). Mainly ex-bourbon, but also ex-sherry and use of Swedish oak.

**McCarthy's Oregon Single Malt** (84.8 proof/42.4%) *Clear Creek Distillery* (Clear Creek, Oregon). Great example of American doing Scottish doing American.

**Millstone 100 Rye** (50%) *Zuidam Distillery* (Zuidam Distillers, Netherlands). Artisanal and detail orientated. The 12 year old malt's just as good.

**Nant 3** (43%) *The Nant Distillery* (Nant Distilling Company, Australia). This or the cask strength equivalent.

**Paul John Peated Select Cask** (55.5%) *John Distilleries* (John Distillers, Ltd). Good example of the newish range of top-ranking Indian single malts.

**St George's Chapter 14** (46%) *St George's Distillery* (English Whisky Co, England). Go for any of their 'chapters'. Clever and farsighted stuff.

**Sullivans Cove Double Cask** (40%) *Tasmania Whisky Distillery* (Sullivan's Cove, Tasmania). Another great Aussie whisky, though pretty pricey, which is why the French oak expression's not here.

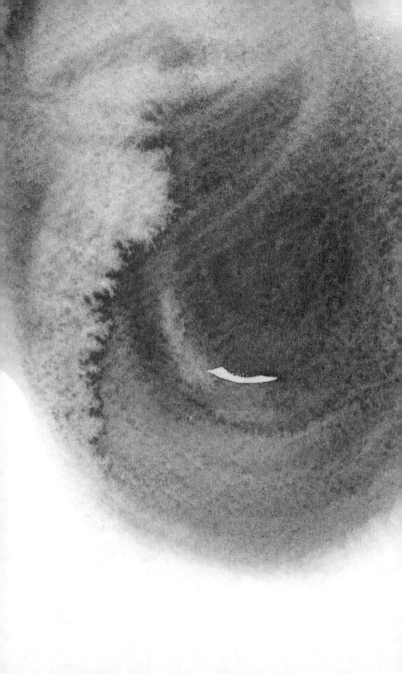

# 11

## BEAUTY BEFORE AGE AND OTHER SURPRISES

Age is no guarantee of quality. A beautiful-tasting whisky may be four years old, a foul-tasting one 21. This is perfectly true, but there's much to unpick. The proliferation of no-age statement (NAS) whiskies remains, for some, a real bone of contention, as do claims for being able to mature whisky more quickly, especially through the use of small casks. Casting its long and influential shadow over both is the boom-specific problem of a shortage of long-aged mature stock.

## BEAUTY BEFORE AGE

Today's sudden and increasing influx of NAS whisky releases is sold on the doubly ironic premise that beauty does after all precede age. Good and great whisky is not, we are told, as heavily hamstrung by time as once thought, many a producer having performed a very modern about-turn, effacing the age statement in favour of all those other factors – technological advances, greater knowledge, better making – that go into the creation of great whisky.

Truth is, the question of age as indicator of quality is indelibly linked to whether or not a distillery possesses ageing stocks. Whisky making is a long haul business. What a producer makes now might not be ready to sell for six, 10, 15 or 20 years – depending on where in the world it ages its stock. That's enough of a wait to break the back of the best of start-ups. It puts enormous pressure on distilleries once silent, the gaps in their liquid archives an impossible fact. And not just (re)start-ups: throughout the industry it becomes an ever pressing issue as demand begins to outstrip supply – as is happening presently.

Exchanging the distiller's hat for an accountant's, the options open to a producer will be dictated largely by the state of its bank balance. Blessed with deep pockets, it might try holding out, hoping to hell that whisky is still the market's favourite once its stock's matured. Otherwise, there are different ways of making money on maturing stock, including selling portions off to independent bottlers, or pawning it out to cash-rich holding companies, or releasing a steady flow of work-in-progress pieces, hints of what's to come, tacit admission that not everything's quite there. Alternatively, there's the NAS option; to think of age as little more than a number, and release the product less an age statement. Playing more and more on the distinction between age and maturity, it's this last option that, in the minds of many, makes most short-term economic sense. Certainly, what was previously a trickle is now a river: the NAS is here to stay – at least for the foreseeable pressurised future.

Thing is, whatever one's views on what makes a whisky mature, age remains an important indicator as to where a whisky might be at any point in the process of maturation. The law mostly dictates that whisky is not whisky before the age of three, and experience suggests that a Scotch or Irish whisky is youthful up to eight years old, begins to deepen at around ten to 12, and reaches special heights there on in, though remains prone to over wooding much after 25 years old. By the same token, though officially itself once in wood for not so long as a day, bourbon is straight when just two years old, youthful up until four, shows signs of maturity at six, is in the zone at eight and is fully grown up at 12, after which the wood is less friend than enemy. Distillers and warehouse managers monitor progress, having an idea, all things fair, of what a whisky will be doing at different age brackets. It's a guide based on years of experience.

Of course, the best of guides allow for the exception, the anomaly, the young pretender. Meaning, just as we parents know to better trust the all-round sangfroid of our 15-year-old over that of our brilliant but still emotionally challenged 21 year old, so the same of whisky. Some whiskies just grow up more quickly than others. Some, like a liquid Buddha, feel ready before they've lived long enough to know any better, while others possess a freshness that utterly belies their super advanced years. I am stretching the analogy. My apologies to all parents: your children are not whisky.

Children or no, these are the exception. Notwithstanding the difference between age and maturity, the fact that an older whisky is not necessarily better than a younger one, there's hardly a producer in the world that, given the stock, will not use age as a primary means of pricing and selling its whisky. Which is not to denigrate excellent, well-balanced NAS whiskies, those that forego statements on the basis that, were they not to do so, then they would have to go with youngest whisky in the blend. Rather it is to highlight their anathema, the growing spate of underdeveloped ones, whiskies that when tasted, taste way too young.

## A LOST CAUSE, SEEMINGLY

Small cask ageing is one of today's white-hot topics and most prominent of the current crop of ideas for cheating time, especially in America, where the burgeoning craft or micro-distilling whisky scene rides a large and complicated wave. Discussions around small cask use are always vociferous, often divisive, occasionally warring. A small number of producers have gone as far as to claim it as ageing's elixir, 18 months in a five, ten or 15 gallon cask as having the equivalent influence on the spirit as five years in a standard size large cask.

Ostensibly, the science behind such claims is relatively easy to follow: the smaller the cask, the greater the ratio of surface (wood) to volume (spirit) contact; this being the case, the smaller the cask, the faster the process of maturation. However, as we already know, maturation is an umbrella term for a number of processes, some of which occur relatively quickly, others over longer time periods. Thus, while a greater ratio of wood to spirit most certainly sees a greater rate of wood extraction over a shorter time, the turbo boost afforded by small barrels leaves less than enough time for the key processes of oxidation and evaporation, the result being a whisky with great colour and lots

## ON CHEATING TIME

We humans have always had a somewhat tricky relationship with time. It moves too fast. It moves too slowly. It just won't be what we want. This being so, we'll do our best to bend it to suit us, with varying results — some double edged. When it comes to maturing stock, there is, says many a distiller, no substitute for time. For others, especially those either caught short or just getting going, squeezing ten years into three is the new Eldorado.

Attempts to speed up maturation are as old as the process itself: the old and sometimes dark arts of spirits rectification take early centre stage, the aim here less to squarely take time on than cheat it altogether. As maturing stock became accepted practice, so methods for either mimicking or fast tracking maturation grew ever more elaborate.

Spirits writer Adam Rogers's *Proof* is very good on this, detailing a long line of time jumpers: the Scots tried soaking the oak in a kind of sherry syrup. Cognac makers employed the now illegal method of heating the eau de vie (distillate) in sealed containers. In keeping with the very earliest of whisky styles, the spirit was flavoured with spices and fruit, while latterly oxygen has been artificially applied to the spirit. Oak chips have been suspended in the liquid. Music played at spirit-agitating low frequencies is claimed by some to make a difference. One company has patented a method that swears by the 'purification' properties of ultrasonic waves. Another even experimented, says Rogers, with sealing casks in plastic. I won't go on. It's a long and awesome list.

of wood, the overriding smoke-hot, tannin-heavy and pine-like tastes indicating signs of a young, possibly immature spirit. If you like it, say its detractors, fair enough, but don't go mistaking it for constituting the properties of a whisky recognised as mature.

Much of the research would seem to back this up. Tannins are by no means fixed. They evolve over time, the not fully understood cataclysmic roles of their derivatives all part of an unfolding set of chemical processes. The breakdown by the spirit of lignen, one of oak's key polymeric structures, sees further low-level flavour producing reactions. Major flavour input comes from the gradual formation and correspondingly incremental increase in the number of oak or so-called 'whisky' lactones, all the result of the effects of oxidation. Acids derived from the wood react to form them, and also esters and other flavour compounds. Simply put, when it comes to maturing whisky, there is no substitute for time, the necessarily late formation of key esters an argument clincher.

## AN APOLOGY FOR THE RELATIVITY OF TIME

The above aside, and though still a minuscule share of the world's output, some very good whisky has been made using small casks. Well thought of, these whiskies – neither over-oaked nor overtly one dimensional – are the whiskies that prove that we have much to learn about the many maturation intricacies of liquid time travel.

It's a huge subject, and impossible to do justice to here, but very briefly: when speaking of small casks, there is clearly a place for them in respect of speeding up the processes of extraction. More, combine small cask physics with the slow motion chemical-bomb potential of a cask that takes into account not just its build, treatment and history, but also choice of oak used, the parts of the tree from which it was constructed, the permeability of the wood and the tightness of its grains, and you begin to make a case for ramping up conditions for oxidation, and therefore for reaction. Add, finally, the influences of an excellent quality new make to considerations as to which level of alcohol to fill the cask at, and we're talking about the possibility of bending time to design.

The success of all this, the prep work, depends entirely on how a distiller chooses to make his or her play. All other things equal, the difference being only cask size, the average producer is more likely to have success with a larger cask, given the depth of our knowledge and the fact of the process having to be less intensively managed. Small cask maturation is a most demanding practice, requiring a much more regular tasting regime, and ought to be seen not as end in itself, but rather as a tool. Generally speaking, those distillers managing to make great whisky using small casks monitor them like hawks. They move the liquid on into both larger or used casks as soon as they deem it ready for new and later forms of maturation. They play to the strengths of their specific warehouse conditions. Less cheating it, they eke speed from time, a warping talent thus far granted the very few.

## FINE EXAMPLES

The following whiskies are the produce of distilleries that go against the age statement grain, having released either NAS and/or relatively young or fast-aged products to acclaim.

**Aberlour a'bunadh** (abv changes with every batch) *Aberlour Distillery* (Chivas Bros–Pernod Ricard, Speyside). Sherry monster – cask strength. Cult following all of its own.

**Ardbeg Uigeadail** (54.2%) *Ardberg Distillery* (Glenmorangie Group, Islay). When speaking of monsters, this one's peated and in the frontline.

**Ardmore Traditional Cask** (46%) *Ardmore Distillery* (Beam Suntory, Highlands). Partially matured in quarter (125 litre/27 gallon) casks.

**Balcones True Blue** (100 proof/50%) *Balcones Distillery* (Balcones Distilling, Texas). Whisky either wholly or partially matured in small casks.

**Dalmore Cigar Malt** (44%) *Dalmore Distillery* (Whyte & Mackay, Highlands). Proper mouth filler. Book in last thing.

**Glenmorangie Signet** (46%) *Glenmorangie Distillery* (Glenmorangie Group, Highlands). Expensive but mainstream classic.

**Hakushu Single Malt Distiller's Reserve** (43%) *Hakushu Distillery* (Suntory). Young and great.

**Laphroaig Quarter Cask** (48%) *Laphroaig Distillery* (Beam Suntory, Islay). 5-year-old whisky part matured in a quarter cask.

**Lark Distillers Selection** (46%) *Lark Distillery* (Lark, Australia). Single 100 litre cask whisky.

**Mackmyra First Edition** (46.1%) *Mackmyra Distillery* (Mackmyra Svensk Whisky, Sweden). Greater proportion made in 100 litre Swedish oak casks.

**Octave and Quarter Cask Range** (46.1%) Limited runs of different unofficial whiskies by independent bottler Duncan Taylor, Scotland. Whiskies all finished in octave (45 litre/10 gallon) or quarter casks. Some very reasonably priced.

**Old Hobart Overeem Port Matured** (43%) *Old Hobart Distillery* (Old Hobart, Tasmania). This and anything else by Casey Overeem, all matured in small casks.

**Taketsuru Pure Malt** (43%). *Miyagikyo Distillery* (Nikka). A wonderful blended malt.

**Talisker 57° North** (57%) *Talisker Distillery* (Diageo, Islands). Wonderful.

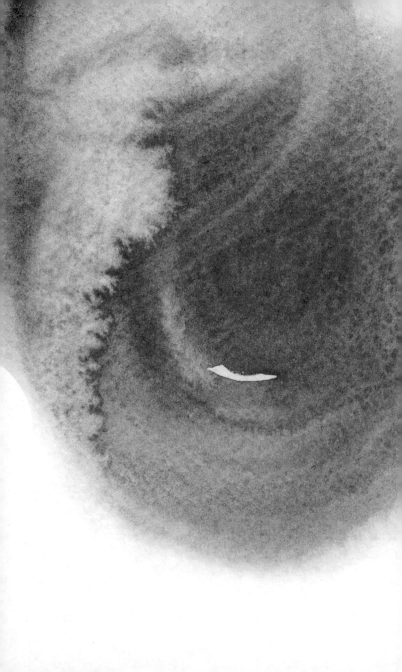

# 12

## A STORM IN A WHISKY GLASS

Drinking and tasting whisky are not always exactly the same thing. Drinking's the main event, and of course doesn't exclude taste, but just as you might enjoy driving a lovely car, it's the overall effect of the experience that matters, not the whys and wherefores, the details, the analysis of the experience. You like the whisky because you like the whisky, period. In which case, there's no good or bad whisky – at least not that we can agree on.

However and hold on: this isn't how things are. Just as you might have taken advice when buying that same lovely car, so you might look to reviews on certain whiskies – as a means of getting some perspective on what's good and what's not. See what you've done? Welcome to the world of the critic, of the tasting note, of criteria, hierarchy and value, an aesthetic of taste, one that, agree or not, appears to champion objective truth over subjective whim.

## FACT OR FANTASY

In wine and spirits, flavour is aroma and taste combined. While it is fairly easy to speak objectively of the primary flavours of the mouth, the immediate taste sensations of bitter, salty, sour, sweet and savoury, and of the various irritating, warming, drying and pungent-like effects of the spirit on the mouth and nasal passages, the aromas smelt both before and during actual tasting are another thing altogether. Numerous and invisible objects, often nameless, and more instantly reminiscent of moments in our past, of a time when we tasted or smelt something just like them, aromas are vehicles into a private world of half-forgotten memories, which when described convey more a poetry of the imagining subject than a language designed to measure and communicate the merits of their source: the whisky itself.

Certainly, this would seem to be the view of Richard E Quandt, economist and author of the cat-among-the-pigeons piece *On Wine Bullshit: Some New Software?*. Quandt takes umbrage with wine tasting on two fronts: the almost universal practice of ranking a wine by a numerical score (usually out of 100, sometimes 10); and the language used to describe its appearance, nose, taste, body, finish and overall balance. The first he describes as being a false measure, a 'bullshit-o-metrics'. The second he calls a 'vocabulary of bullshit', a given set of tasting notes so subjective as to be no more useful than a randomly selected list of descriptors – as generated by a piece of software. What exactly, he asks, is ultra-silky tannin?

While Quandt's sights are set on the world of wine, Chuck Cowdery gives scoring whiskies similar short thrift in his analysis *Why Ratings are Bull*. Publications are forced, he says, to numerically rate whiskies, 'producers and their advertisers' being much fonder of the impression of immutable quality as presumed by a number than they are of the editorial vagaries of written review. By its nature a group of individuals, a given panel of judges, is rarely fixed or consistent. Personnel change, as do tastes, and so a review is what it is: the subjective opinion of an individual. Besides, unless a consumer's aware of the publication's guidelines, scores of 79 plus will always feel high. It's not really out of 100. It's a competiton between good, better and best.

Speaking of subjectivity, it would seem that we are biologically determined to create a private tasting language. As Adam Rogers says in *Proof*, the majority of us can identify up to four aromas – say chocolate, smoke, cheese and sulphur – with reasonable consistency, especially after some training. Complicate things much more, however, throw in two or more flavour compounds, combine them in different ways, and our ability to spot that which we confidently identified only seconds ago is reduced to nothing. 'After four different smells, the human basically chunks them all together', forming a 'gestalt aroma' that 'becomes the identifying aroma for that object'. In other words, we invent our own personal aromas.

It gets worse: as well as invent, we are also hoodwinked – by sight, no less. Again, much of the work on this has been done in wine, where famously it has been shown how a few drops of flavourless red dye can fool a master of wine into tasting flavours typical of a red in what in fact is a white. The nose is bushwhacked by a mirage. This is taste analysis at the bottom of a large hole.

## TOWARDS A SCIENCE OF TASTING

For the likes of Quandt, an objective sensory analysis of whisky is nearly impossible. If we're going to say anything, he says, then keep it simple, and make sure it's something we all agree on: that is, colour plus indisputable basic flavour descriptors (bitter, sweet etc.) plus that which is truly measurable (length of finish, for example). That way, we keep the bullshit to the absolute minimum.

I like a lot of what Quandt has to say, though perhaps not for exactly the same reasons. Certainly, opinion masquerading as fact is wrong. It makes gatekeepers and impenetrable rituals out of something that ought to be open to all: the joys of taste, the pleasurable effects of ethanol.

However, while it's interesting – and something of a relief – to note that even a master of wine is fallible, it doesn't necessarily follow that everything he or she has ever said is without merit. Given the right conditions, it's possible to trick or break almost anyone. It seems that the colour red acts as a cue for sweetness, thereby influencing sense of taste *before* the act of actually tasting. We see red: we taste the properties of red. As a synaesthete might say, nothing's guaranteed.

Truth is, and notwithstanding the private and hallucinatory world of sensual perception, there's no substitute when it comes to knowledge and experience. While no one's clear about everything, there are objectively identifiable reasons for the existence of certain aromas. It's not so much that they do not exist, but rather how to recognise – and so speak about - them. The onus, then, is on producers, tasters and critics to communicate what they know using an established set of rules, and to keep to what they can taste. Do so and we allow, as we

## MAPPING FLAVOUR

Based on a history of odour classification, and especially on the beer and wine flavour wheels of Morten Meilgaard and Ann Noble, whisky has made use of a variety of sophisticated flavour guides. Some are industry facing, their function a tool for professional tasters, whose job it is to evaluate batches of newly matured whisky against previous same-brand releases. Others have evolved as blending aids. Many function as consumer-friendly infographs. The best speak a language designed to communicate real knowledge.

As an example, one of the most detailed flavour whisky infographs is Scotch Whisky Research Institute's revised wheel, which divides aroma and 'flavour by mouth' into 14 primary descriptors, each of which is further divided into a set of secondary descriptors. Thus, 'primary taste' breaks down into sweet, sour, salty and bitter. 'Phenolic', meanwhile, divides into medicinal, peaty and kippery; 'mouthfeel effects', mouth coating, astringent and mouth warming; 'feints', leathery, tobacco, sweat and stale fish – and so on. While not universal ('kipper' is nothing to someone who has no idea what a kipper is), and always evolving, these are real words, and serve as a means of sharing the invisible.

shall see, for both the subjective *and* the objective. Thus, while it's perfectly possible to make use of descriptors lifted from everyday speech, or use memory, simile or metaphor in order to give voice to the otherwise private, the nuts and bolts of what is said can be shown to have a proper scientific basis.

## FROM BULLSHIT TO HYPOTHESIS

So, when nosing a whisky, and you find yourself, Proustian-like, catapulted back to the sight of your mother's nails, the smell of glue in the air, be at peace. No need to book an appointment with your therapist. You may think or note, 'mum's nails, dressing table, gown, the house on Hanover Square', which is fine and fun and enough to drive Quandt wild. If pressed, however, you may define the memory as meaning a note of nail polish remover, which in turn might indicate that certain acetates – methyl and ethyl – formed during fermentation have been allowed to survive the effects of distillation and of maturation. If more than a note, then it might even mean that fusel alcohols created during fermentation have so dominated the beer's amino acids as to result in a solvent-heavy wash, an imbalance possibly exacerbated by a too early first cut, and then underlined or consolidated when laid down in poor wood, and for not long enough. Conclusion: it's a tainted whisky – perhaps. There's a method to the bullshit.

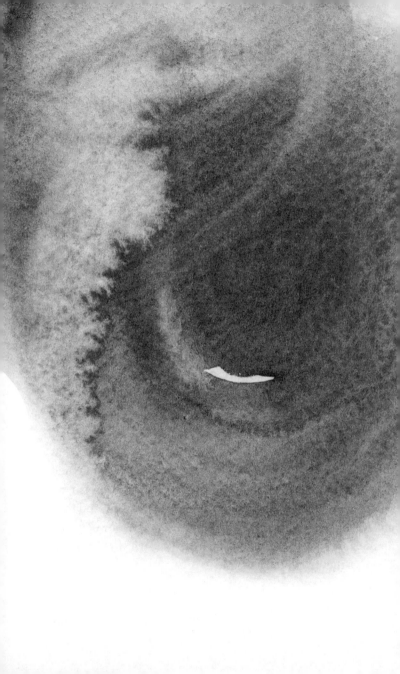

# 13

## A ROUGH GUIDE TO DRINKING WHISKY

This could be the shortest guide in whisky: enjoy it how you like. Whisky's not about white men, or old men, or even just men. Women drink it, and women make it. So do African Americans, Indians, the Taiwanese. It's as Japanese as it is Scottish, as urban as it is rural. It's light, it's heavy, it's versatile. It's an aperitif, an evening starter, an after-dinner nightcap. It's drunk neat. It's drunk with water. It's drunk with soda, ginger ale and cola. Green tea's the rage in Asia, coconut water in Brazil. The late Elmer T Lee took his bourbon with a dash of Sprite. And he was the Master Distiller Emeritus at Buffalo Trace Distillery, Kentucky – and white, and old, and a man.

## THE TRUTH, THE WHOLE TRUTH AND NOTHING BUT THE TRUTH, SO HELP ME GOD

Ostensibly, the label on a bottle is a statement of identity. Exactly what it has to tell you about itself will depend on the laws of either its country of origin or those in its countries of export. Generally, it gives the bottle's contents a name, a type, the producer and the alcoholic strength. It may give an area, cask details, the dates of distillation and bottling, and even, as is true of Japanese products, the owner of the non-independent distillery.

Labels do not by law have to give an age statement, except in the case of an under four-year-old bourbon. If the label does carry an age statement, then the age refers to the youngest whisky in the blend. If it doesn't, then the minimum age will be guaranteed by its country of origin's definition of what constitutes whisky – normally three years. Age, of course, is no guarantee of quality, but careful: while a very good NAS whisky demonstrates beautifully the fallacy of mistaking age for maturity, NAS whiskies breed like it's spring during times when producers are low on middle to old-aged stock. With distilleries opening left, right and centre, and shortage scares the order of the day, now is such a time.

Of course, unless clear as to the history of a particular producer or whisky, or indeed aware of the difference between official and unofficial bottlings, the information on your labels can confuse. Producers label what they have to and advertise what sells. A single barrel or cask strength whisky will certainly advertise itself as such, as will a small-batch, non-filtered, naturally coloured one. If not a sales lifter, if, for example, a non-producing distiller (NPD) selling bought-in whisky under its own name, then it's an unusually candid company that reveals its whisky source, a particularly thorny American issue, with NPDs making the most of legislation that allows companies to label themselves as producers of product they have only packaged. If no mention of natural colouring or non-chill filtering, then place those bets: it's probably coloured and chill-filtered. If 'handcrafted' or any other hard-to-pin-down descriptors of the moment, then know that you may now be at the copywriter's desk. It's a minefield. Do your research. Buy with knowledge.

Whisky, unlike wine, ceases to age once bottled. There is some change, but so little as to be almost imperceptible. The Shackleton whiskies recently unearthed in Antarctica were 100 plus years in the bottle and tasted, by all accounts, very good. Whisky lasts, especially high-strength whisky. However, once opened, the influx of oxygen into more and more headspace will act as a catalyst for chemical change. One or two whisky heads advise that it ought to be polished off within six months to a year – either that or transferred to a smaller bottle. Whisky bottles are generally screw cap, though a producer may use cork, usually as a point of difference.

## WHEN TASTING WHISKY

With whisky on the perennial up, tastings these days are held everywhere – bars, pubs, clubs, parties, festivals. Ubiquitous and often a great introduction to new expressions, nobody I know tastes whisky in exactly the same way, though fair to say the process will normally mean looking at it, then nosing, tasting and either spitting or swallowing it. With a few tips and a bit of practice, there's no reason why any of us can't do the same.

### APPEARANCE
While much is – or has been – made of colour, it's not true to say that a deep orange looking whisky will taste better than one that looks like a watered down bottle of lemon squash. Wood gives

# INDEPENDENT BOTTLERS

Occasionally you will come across a whisky produced by an independent bottler. The independent bottler rarely owns the distilleries that made the whisky it sells. Nor is it a newly founded distillery buying in stock while waiting for its own to mature. Rather, it buys up casks of surplus or interesting stock, which it sells on, normally at highly competitive prices, either at different bottling ages or having further blended and / or aged the whisky itself. Distilleries sell stock because they have to or because they've arranged to.

Though by no means always the case, independent bottlers often specialise in buying up mothballed or dismantled distillery stocks. Many contract individual distilleries to age a portion of the distillate in their own specially chosen barrels. Others age the distillate in their own warehouses, in their own barrels. The independent bottler's point of difference is difference itself. It is niche. It deals in small and rare runs, runs never to be repeated. Its products are by definition unofficial bottlings. In the vast majority of cases, it reveals the source of its whisky, and will often go beyond simply acknowledging the distillery, detailing cask size, type and number, as well as dates of distillation and bottling.

the spirit its colour, and a used cask will colour its contents less than a virgin oak cask. Meanwhile, the level of viscosity – the syrupiness of its 'legs' – is evidence of body, and so perhaps of strength, though not of its overall quality. There's a lot to be read into the appearance of a whisky, but it's just the cover. Open it. Smell it. Drink it.

## NOSING

When nosing, you can use any glass you like, but the funnelling effects of those with smaller lip-circumference gives better access to evaporating aromas. If your nose prickles, then that's the ethanol, which will affect your ability to smell. Lift your head, nose and, once tasted, add some water. Nose it again.

And take your time. The flavours in a given whisky will naturally unlock over a period much longer than it would ordinarily take to drink it. As said, most of us are only capable of identifying a couple of aromas in any one go. And we tire of the same smell. Give the whisky a rest. As it warms and aerates, so its flavour profile evolves, the lightest evaporating flavour compounds making way for heavier ones. Meanwhile, the added water frees cogeners previously locked in clumping molecules of ethanol.

A professional taster's notes may read as if the whole process has taken about five minutes. Don't be fooled. Keep coming back, even after other whiskies have been tasted. If you like, make some notes along the way – emotional, metaphorical or literal.

## CHOOSING YOUR WHISKY

When choosing what to taste, think in terms of groups or 'flights' of whisky – between three and five. These can be anything you like, though as you get into it, comparing and contrasting according to category makes for interesting experiments.

To start, then, try comparing different styles – single malt, grain, bourbon or Irish pot still. Further, you might set pot against column, one grain against another, American oak versus European. Equally, you could compare different whiskies matured in the same type of oak. If in search of single variable differences, then the mind boggles: different distilleries, finishes, mashbills, yeasts, strengths, types of warehouse, age. The main thing: enjoy.

## TASTING

Take two sips. The first sets the mouth, the second's what counts. When it comes to imbibing, you're on borrowed time. Anything over 25% abv will progressively affect your ability to actually taste the whisky. Plus, your judgement will deteriorate the more you drink. If swallowing, all advice points to you sticking at between three and six whiskies. I find the law of diminishing returns kicks in at about number four. You may be different. You may be an ox.

When tasting, keep the liquid in your mouth long enough for things to settle. Move it about the mouth. Don't look for separate primary taste areas – it's much more of a jumble in there than previously thought. Think about flavour physically and aromatically. If you catch and image or name a scent, then great, note it down. Alternatively, think about how the whisky feels. It could feel dry. It may grip, feel bitter or pulse through the mouth. There may be a hint of fire, a warming, hot, even peppery feel – as in mild chilli, ginger or even strong menthol chewing gum. Add water and see what happens. Again, make notes.

## FINISH

Swallow and wait. The finish is all about what's left, the aftertaste – its presence, the flavour, and how long it lasts. Some whiskies last a long time once gone. Some punch out, or disappear in waves. Others the mouth hardly remembers. The finish rounds off the tasting experience.

## MAKING SENSE OF YOUR NOTES

Apart from the fun of it, you might be interested in giving your observations a slightly more concrete context. If so, and you've made notes, then try matching them to whatever flavour guide you have at hand. Some of the words used will be exactly the same as those on the chart, meaning you've hit the nail on the scientific head. Others you'll have to best-fit. Any simile or metaphor you'll decipher or discard – or keep as is, it seeming to capture perfectly an essential poetic truth.


# THE FREEDOM TO MIX

A confession. When I started drinking whisky, I believed the only way was neat. Persuaded of the flavour-enhancing benefits of water, I relented, but only slightly. Just a drop, please – and no thank you to ice, soda or anything sweet, which I thought of as a cop-out, a mask. I was quietly, politely insufferable. I'd like to say I've changed – as a person – now that I've seen the light. My wife knows differently. Nevertheless, I was led to the trough, and I did drink.

When mixing whisky, water is your first and last port of call. 'Water', says Dave Broom, 'is your friend'. It can rescue an average whisky, enhance an excellent one and help save your oesophagus. It will rarely ruin a whisky. It's up to you, but I would advise adding a few drops to anything over 50% abv – as much for the good of your health as for helping release flavour. Exceptions that prove the rule: when drinking not to taste, but rather just for pleasure, you may find watering down below 40% introduces a previously undetected bitterness, knocking the whisky off balance. Occasionally, an old and delicate whisky won't suffer dilution.

Ice, meanwhile, has the opposite effect to water. Whereas water will open up a whisky, ice closes it down. In the case of a strong whisky, this might be just the ticket. It will reduce nasal and mouth burn. It does, however, slow down rates of evaporation, meaning less on the nose. The pay cheque's an initial refreshingly cool mouthfeel, followed by an explosion of flavour as the mouth warms the aromatic molecules. Finally, if you happen across a bartender who practises the Japanese bar art of carving the ice into a large ball, dropping it in a tumbler, and pouring the whisky over the top, then try it – at least once.

To end, bubbles and our first official cocktail: a whisky with soda. Apart from sharing all of water's aforementioned attributes, the bubbles in carbonated water aren't nearly as benign as they might first appear. They stimulate the tongue – in a similar irritating fashion that chilli or menthol does. They're slightly acidic. They're dry and at the same time freshening. Small ones help taxi aromatic molecules up and out towards the nose. If you're having one, a tip: take advice. Not every whisky works well with soda. Some pairings bring a bitter element to the drink, others were born to meet. If you've never tried a whisky highball, then here's your super crisp start.

## BAR, COCKTAILS AND A BITE TO EAT

The bar – and its tender – is whisky's frontline; its theatre, the place it gets to act out, to mix with its extended family, to compete with its own kind. Any whisky bar worth its salt will have a busy back shelf, the head bartender the librarian responsible for the quality of its collection. Here's where you go to taste what's out there, what's new, different, lost or really and truly ought to be tried. It's the most wonderful of multisensory classrooms, your bartender both guide and fellow explorer. It should not intimidate, and if it does, then there are plenty of bars in the sea.

Having taken some time to persuade the cocktail world of its versatility, whisky's very much at the forefront of an industry that as well as playing guardian to the classics has brought a Fat Duck-type experimentalism to the art of mixed drinks making. Certainly, whether technically fantastical or old school simple, the cocktail has introduced new generations to the joys of whisky, not least in 1990s Japan, where the highball singlehandedly brought it back from the brink. Note, contrary to received opinion, it's not just about the blends and those easier going bourbons. Depending on what you go with, single malts are eminently mixable.

Away from the bar and high stool, whisky is unlikely anytime soon to topple wine as food's great accompanier, for the simple reason of it being so strong. This said, as the phenomenal successes of both the mizuwari (ice, water, whisky, long glass) and the highball in Japan show, never say never: diluted and drunk long, it may yet have its day. For now, however, where food's concerned, whisky in the wider world of eating out continues to suffer something of a pufferfish complex: fatal (to food taste buds) unless matched by a world class expert. Not true. Depending on style and strength, whisky goes very well with lots of sweet foods, most things fish, red meat, a whole raft of cheeses and anything you might consider powerful tasting – though not 70% plus cocoa chocolate, more palate cleaner than partner. Whisky and food: do try this at home.

## LUDWIG'S LAST WORD

So, whisky: there's truth and there's you, the interpreter of that truth. Meaning, I'm having it both ways. Objectively, whisky making's no perfect science, but science there is, which is why we can agree to talk about good and bad whiskies. However, it's actually about you and what you like. As the philosopher Ludwig Wittgenstein might say, reading this book's been a ladder climb, but now you're here, on the roof, there's no need for it. Kick the ladder away. Enjoy whisky as you like – neat, with water, ice, bubbles, a mixer that suits. Remember also that you are, in the eyes of the whisky producer, both a human and a sales number. No need to be suspicious, or go to war, or start your own distillery, but don't just rely on the label. Do your research. Trust your palate. In the end, it really is about you. Have enormous fun.

## FINE EXAMPLES

The following cocktails are selected to show the range and versatility of whisky with various mixers.

**Bobby Burns** Like a Manhattan with scotch, use the fruitiness of 2 parts of Johnny Walker Gold, 1/4 part sweet vermouth and 1 teaspoon of Benedictine in place of the bitters.

**Fancy Scotch Mist** Fantastically simple. Laphroaig 10, sugar and Fees Bros whisky barrel-aged bitters. Swizzle in a small glass with crushed ice until frosty and garnish with a lemon twist.

**The Penicillin** Contemporary classic, invented in 2005 by Sam Ross. 2 parts blended scotch, 1/4 part Islay Single Malt, lemon, honey and ginger syrup, shaken and served on the rocks.

**Boulevardier** Similar to a negroni, for extra spice try 1 part Rittenhouse 100, 1 part Campari and 1 part sweet vermouth.

**East Meets West** 9 parts Cardhu 12, 1 part Talisker 10, 2 parts sake, 2 parts port, 1 part sugar. Stirred, strained and poured over an ice ball, with a shiso leaf to garnish.

**Freakishly Fabulous Fascinating Fig Fashioned** A double Auchentoshan Three Wood, 3 teaspoons of cream fig jam and 1 teaspoon of green chartreuse. Mix and throw, fine strain on the rocks, and garnish with a lemon twist.

# WHISKY SPEAK

An A–Z of useful whisky words, terms and abbreviations.

**Angel's Share** The name for the liquid lost to evaporation during maturation.

**ABV** Alcohol by volume.

**Beer** The fermented liquid – also known as the wash.

**Blend** Term used to describe mixing or vatting whisky, either more of the same or different types.

**Blended whisky** A whisky made by the vatting together of two or more whiskies. In Scotland, must be sourced from different distilleries to qualify as a blended scotch, a blended grain or a blended malt.

**Bond** Where whisky is held in storage - i.e. the warehouse - before excise duty is paid.

**Bottled in Bond** A whisky on which excise duty's been paid. In America it is also a 4 year old plus 50% abv whisky taken from one distilling season, made by one distiller at a single distillery.

**Bourbon** One of the four whisky styles. Must be made in America, from majority corn.

**Caramel** / E150. Used to artificially colour whisky. Said to be flavourless, but controversial in that its use panders to the erroneous belief that whisky ought to be a certain colour to be considered good whisky.

**Cask** Another name for barrel – used to mature spirit.

**Cask strength** A whisky taken from usually multiple casks and bottled without having been first diluted with water.

**Charred** As in the inside of a cask having been burnt – a process involving direct fire. It has a positive effect on the maturing whisky.

**Chill filtered** Procedure by which a whisky is chilled, the resultant clumping of fatty acids etc. filtered through a wire mesh. Controversial process designed to stop the whisky clouding – thought to affect taste.

**Column still** Also known as Coffey, continuous and patent still. A still used to distil spirits continuously. Used throughout the world, though especially in America and Canada.

**Cooper** Makes casks. Place of work is a cooperage.

**Distillation** Method by which alcohol in a beer or the equivalent is concentrated through a process of evaporation and condensation.

**Dram** A shot of whisky – Scottish.

**Feints** The third and unusable part of the spirit run. Also called 'tails'. Recycled into the next wash.

**Fermentation** Process by which yeast converts sugar to alcohol, mainly ethanol and traces of other chemical compounds.

**Foreshots** The first and unusable part of the spirit run. Also called 'heads'. Recycled into the next wash.

**Grain whisky** One of the four styles of whisky, made from unmalted grains, usually corn, wheat or rye.

**Grist** Ground grain, a mix of flour and husk.

**Heart** The middle and usable part of the spirit run. Also known as the 'middle cut'. This is the 'new make', which is then matured as whisky.

**Irish pot still** One of the four styles of whisky; made from a mashbill of barley and malted barley.

**Kiln** Room or zone for hot air drying malting grain – usually barley. It halts germination and has the effect of either subtly or obviously adding flavour to the grain.

**Low wines** The distillate taken from the wash still – the first distillation in the distillation process, its strength being around 23 abv.

**Lyne arm** A longish copper tube / 'arm' running off – and roughly perpendicular to - the top of the pot still, and through which the evaporated alcohol flows into the condenser.

**Mash** The result of grain(s) being mixed or cooked with hot water.

**Mashbill** Identified portions of types of grains added to the mash.

**Mash tun** A vessel used for making the mash or wort.

**Malt** Partially germinated barley.

**Malt whisky** One of the four styles of whisky; made from malted grain, usually barley.

**NAS** No-age statement. Describes a whisky that does not reveal its age.

**New make** Name given to the spirit or distillate prior to being matured.

**NPD** Non-producing distillery. American term used to describe producers that do not produce their own whisky.

**Oxidation** The catalytic effect of oxygen during maturation.

**Peat** Old, decomposed vegetation traditionally used as fuel for the purpose of kilning the malting barley. Added bonus of imparting flavour.

**Pot still** Traditional alembic still. Mandatory in Scotland for the making of malt whisky. Used also in Ireland, Japan, Europe and to a lesser extent America, Canada and the rest of the world.

**Reflux** Process by which alcohol vapour condenses and falls back into the pot before reaching or escaping down the lyne arm. Added reflux makes for a lighter spirit.

**Shell and tube** A modern type of condenser, the 'shell' being the container holding rows upon rows of water-cooled copper tubing – 'tube' – through which the alcohol vapour runs, and which has the effect of condensing it into new make spirit.

**Single cask / barrel** A whisky matured in a single barrel, then bottled without having been blended (mixed) with any other casks or barrels.

**Single malt** A malt whisky made in a single distillery. As opposed to a 'blended malt', which is a blended whisky of two or more malts, usually taken from two or more distilleries.

**Small batch** An undefined term describing – suggesting – a whisky on a less than industrial scale. Being an unregulated descriptor, 'small' is a relative term.

**Sour mash** A portion of the used or spent mash recycled into the incoming mash. Also known as 'backset'. Used in much American straight whisky making.

**Spirit still** The still used to distil the low wines, the second part of the process of double distillation. Also known as the 'low wines' still.

**Toasted** As in the inside of a cask having been toasted – a process involving indirect heat. Like charring, it has a positive effect on the maturing whisky.

**Triple distilled** Process of distillation that sees the heart of the second distillation carried through to a third distillation, the heads and tails from each spirits distillation recycled into the next incoming batch.

**Vatted – or pure – malt** Two no longer legal terms for 'blended malt', descriptors many feel make much more sense, certainly in terms of distinguishing the product from blended Scotch whisky.

**Wash** Distiller's beer.

**Washback** Fermenting vessel.

**Wash still** The still used to distil the 'wash' or beer, the first part of the process of double distillation.

**Worm tub** Traditional condenser. A copper tube snakes or 'worms' its way through a tub of water, the water condensing the vapour flowing through it.

**Wort** Sugary liquid resulting from the mash.

# FURTHER READING

If your interest has been piqued by this little book, then I most humbly recommend the following.

## BOOKS
– *The World Atlas of Whisky* and *Whisky: The Manual* (Dave Broom, Mitchell Beazley, 2014). I make no apologies for referencing each of these heavily in my own writing. Broom's *Atlas* is a masterpiece in flavour understanding, his *Manual* a gateway to the versatility of whisky.
– *Bourbon Straight* (Chuck Cowdery, Made and Bottled in Kentucky, 2004) and *Bourbon Strange* (Chuck Cowdery, Made and Bottled, 2014). Again, Cowdery is someone I go to time and again, his ability to stand and shout at the world completely unassisted ably matched by a talent for telling true stories very well.
– *Whisky: The Definitive World Guide* (Michael Jackson and contributors, Dorling Kindersley, 2005). Manages everything: it's approachable, technical and beautifully written.
– *Canadian Whisky: The Portable Expert* (Davin de Kergommeaux, McClelland & Stewart, 2012). Want to see whisky through the eyes of someone who loves it with his whole being? Read this. Canadian whisky owes de Kergommeaux a life supply of the stuff.
– *World Whisky* (Charles Maclean and contributors, Dorling Kindersley, 2009). Covers a great deal – everything from production to style to bottle design, but especially good for the story behind each whisky featured.
– *Whisky: Technology, Production and Marketing* (Inge Russell et al., Elsevier, 2003). A set of heavy duty papers by a set of heavy duty writers. If you're going to make your own, or want to see whisky through a pair laboratory goggles, then here's where you start, work and finish.
– *The Science and Commerce of Whisky* (Ian Buxton and Paul S. Hughs, The Royal Society of Chemistry Publishing, 2014). The clue's all in the publishing name, though there's everything here: history, flavour making and branding, all under one roof.

– *Proof: The Science of Booze* (Adam Rogers, Houghton Mifflin Harcourt, 2014). A personal journey through the ins and outs of booze, Rogers's talent for making the molecular entertaining is a boon to the non-scientist reader.

– *Malt Whisky Yearbook* (Ingvar Ronde et al., MagDig). If you want to keep up with all things malt, then this yearly book is it: a highly approachable set of opening articles, an A–Z of malt distilleries and contributing commentaries from around the world.

## BLOGS

There are hundreds of really good whisky blogs out there, 99.9% recurring of which I'll have to leave for you to discover. In the meantime, here's where I go to learn:

– *Whisky Science* (whiskyscience.blogspot.co.uk) What it says on the tin. An excellent resource for, as it advertises itself, 'bits of information about Scotch whisky, production, history and chemistry.'

– *Sku's Recent Eats* (recenteats.blogspot.co.uk). A great, opinionated and wide-ranging read – he is also a compulsive compiler of lists, so as well as distilleries, he's vetted a whole heap of other blogs.

– *The Chuck Cowdery Blog* (chuckcowdery.blogspot.co.uk). Kicks corporate ass in the name of you, the consumer, applying the insider-outsider skills of a copywriter turned writer to brilliant and amusing effect.

– *Diving For Pearls* (thekrav.blogspot.co.uk). Michael Kravitz. A one man super-reviewer of (in the main) malt, he's fast and feisty and very much into his numbers.

– *Malt Madness* (maltmadness.com). The nutter(s )who started it all, home also to Malt Maniac Archive and Whisky Fun. What it doesn't know and say about malt... A one-stop shop for everything, from distillery to epistle to the unapologetically obscure.

– *Nonjatta* (nonjatta.com). Chris Bunting and friends' blog is renowned for being the last English word on all things Japanese whisky.

# INDEX

Aberlour a'bunadh 128
acids 33, 39, 126
aftertaste 146
Alberta Premium Dark
   Horse 108
aldehydes 33, 38–9
American whiskies 11–12,
   28, 51, 112–17
   straight 51, 72
   see also bourbon;
   Tennessee whisky
Amrut Fusion 116
'angel's share' 38, 43
Antiquary 12, The 54
Ardbeg 10 66
Ardbeg Uigeadail 128
Ardmore Traditional Cask
   128

'backset' 25
Balcones 113
   Balcones Crooked Texas
     Straight Bourbon 116
   Balcones Texas Single
     Malt 112
   Balcones True Blue 128
Ballantine's 17 54
Balvenie Portwood 21 66
barley
   malted 15, 16, 22–3, 34
   unmalted 16–17, 34
Battle Point Organic
   Washing Whisky 116
Beam Suntory 71, 74, 97
beer 10–11, 25
Belgian Owl Single Malt 116
Benromach 10 66
Black Bull 12, The 54
Black Grouse 54
Blanton's Original Single
   Barrel 76
blended whiskies 29, 46–55
   Scotch 51, 60–61, 64
Blue Hanger 54
Bobby Burns 151
Boece, Hector 58
Booker's 76
Boulevardier 151
bourbon 13, 15–16, 24, 25,
   35, 41, 46, 70–77, 122
Bowmore 12 66

Broom, Dave 10, 13, 59, 91,
   93, 147
Brown Forman 71
Buchanans 61
buckwheat 34
Bulleit Bourbon 76
Bushmills 90, 94, 97
   Bushmills Black Bush 98
   Bushmills Malt 98

Canadian Club Chairman's
   Select 100 Rye Whisky
   108
Canadian whiskies 18, 28,
   51, 102–9
Caola Ila 12 66
caramel(s) 29, 38
Caribou Crossing Single
   Barrel 108
casks, oak 28–9, 37–9
   and evaporation 43
   making 39
   moving into different 42
   small cask ageing 123,
     126–7
   toasting and charring
     39, 41
   used and unused 41
Chichibu Peated 86
chill filtering 29
clouding 29
Clynelish 66
cocktails 148, 149, 151
Coffey Grain Whisky 86
Coffey stills 93; see column
   stills
cogeners 33, 36, 144
Colonel EH Taylor
   Small Batch 77
colour(ing) 29, 142, 144
column stills 27, 28
Connemara 12 Peated 98
copper: and flavour 36
Cor, Brother John 11, 58
corn 34
corn whisky 18
Corsair Triple Smoke 116
Cowdery, Chuck 73, 133
craft distilleries 114
Craigellachie 13 66
Crown Royal XO 108
Crown Royal Hand Selected
   Barrel 108
Cutty Sark 18 54

Dalmore Aurora 6–7
Dalmore Cigar Malt 128
Dewar (John) & Son 61
   Dewar's 18 55
Diageo 13, 63, 65, 97
Dickel, George 71
distillation 25, 28, 36–7
dunnage warehouses 42, 43

East Meets West 151
esters 33, 39
ethanol 6, 12, 33, 37, 38, 144
evaporation 38, 43

Fancy Scotch Mist 151
fermentation 24–5, 33
food: and whisky 149–50
Forty Creek John's Private
   Cask No 1 108
Four Roses 71, 74
   Four Roses Single Barrel
     76
Freakishly Fabulous
   Fascinating Fig
   Fashioned 151

Gibson's Finest Rare 18 109
Glenfiddich 65
   Glenfiddich 18 67
Glengoyne 49–50
Glenlivet 65
   Scotch Ushers Old Vatted
     Glenlivet 61
Glenmorangie Signet 129
grain whisky 13, 17–18,
   23–4, 25, 46
grains 32, 34–5
   peating 33
   roasting 32–3
Green Spot 98
Greenlees Bros 61
Greenore 8 98
grist mills 23

Haig Dimple 15 55
Hakushu 83, 84, 85
   Hakushu 12 86
Hanyu whisky 84
Heaven Hill 71, 96
Hedonism 55
Hibiki 21 86
higher alcohols 33
Highland Park 21 67
Highwood Ninety 20 109

independent bottlers 143
Irish pot still whisky 13,
  16–17, 25, 46, 92
Irish whiskies 11–12, 51,
  90–99, 121

Jameson Special Reserve
  12 98
Japanese whiskies 15, 51,
  80–87, 112
Johnny Drum Private
  Stock 77
Johnnie Walker 61
  Johnnie Walker Black
  Label 55

Karuizawa 1981–1984 86
Kavalan Single Malt 116
Kilbeggan 15 98
Koval Single Barrel Bourbon
  117

labels 95, 140–41
Laddie 10, The 67
Lagavulin 16 67
Laphroaig 10 67
Laphroaig Quarter Cask 129
Lark Distillers Selection 129
Lee, Elmer T. 140
Lot 40 109
low wines 25

Macallan 65
MacBeathads, the 10
McCarthy's Oregon Single
  Malt 117
Mackie & Co. 61
Mackinlay's The Journey 55
Mackmyra Brukswhisky 117
Mackmyra First Edition 129
Maker's Mark 74
malt whiskies 13, 15, 25,
  33, 46
  single 46, 53, 63, 64,
  65, 112
malting barley 22–3
Mars Malt: The Revival 87
'mash' 15, 24, 25, 33
  spent mash 25
mashbills 23, 35
mash tun 23
Mastersons 10 Year Old
  Straight Rye 109

maturation, rates of 42,
  124–5
MGP Indiana 71
micro distilleries 104, 112,
  113
Midleton 90, 93, 94, 96, 97
  Midleton Very Rare 98
millet 34
Millstone 100 Rye 117
mixing whisky 147–8
  see also cocktails
Miyagikyo 10 87

Nant 3 117
NAS (no age statement)
  whiskies 120–23, 141
new make 25
new world whismies 114–15
Nikka 83, 85
  Nikka Coffee Malt Whisky
  87
  Nikka Whisky From the
  Barrel 87
  The Nikka 12, 87
Noah's Mil 77
nosing 137, 144
NPDs (non producing
  distillers) 141

oak, flavours of 40
  see also casks, oak
oats 34
Oban 14 67
O'Cathain, Aine 10
Octave and Quarter Cask
  Range 129
Old Forester Birthday
  Bourbon 77
Old Hobart Overeem Port
  Matured 129
Old Pulteney 17 67

peating grains 33
Penicillin, The 151
Pernod Ricard 63, 97
pot stills 25, 26, 28
Powers Gold Label 99
'proof' 13

Quandt, Richard E. 133,
  134–5
quinoa 34

racked warehouses 42, 43
Redbreast 12 99
Rittenhouse Straight Rye 77
Rogers, Adam 125, 134
Royal Salute 21 55
rye 15, 34
rye whisky 18

St George's Chapter 14 117
Scotch whiskies 12, 58–67,
  121
'setback' 25
single malts see malt
  whiskies
spelt 34
Springbacnk 10 67
Stagg, George T 74, 76
Stein, Robert 28
stills 25–8, 36
strength, measuring 12–13
Sullivans Cove Double
  Cask 117
sulphuric flavours 33, 36
Suntory 51, 80, 83, 84, 85

Taketsuru, Masataka 82–3
Taketsuru 17 87
Talisker 67, 129
tannins 40, 41, 126
tasting, whisky 132–7, 142,
  144, 145, 146–7
Teeling 90, 97
  Teeling Single Grain 99
  Teeling Single Malt 99
Tennessee whisky 14, 18, 70
Torii, Shinjiro 82
Tyrconnell Sherry Cask 99

vanilla/vanillin 40, 41

warehouses 42, 43
'wash' 25
washbacks 24
Weller, W L 12
wheat 34
Wild Turkey 71
  Wild Turkey 101 77
Wiser's 18 109
wort 23, 24, 25

Yamazaki 82, 84, 85
  Yamazaki 18 87
  Yamazaki Sherry Cask 80
yeast, distiller's 24

# ACKNOWLEDGEMENTS

Any writing involves other people. I'm surprised at this. I like to imagine it's an unrelentingly solitary occupation. Far from it, and especially in respect of this little book, for which I owe many people a lot, a debt my gratitude hardly begins to repay. Still, let's begin with that.

Thank you: Johnny Ray, great pal, and the reason why I made that first trip to Iceland. Dave Broom, for taking a punt on an only slightly younger me, his endless patience, his advice, and for being my first reader. Peter Grogan, for the nod. Marcin Miller, always so kind, and a great waver of magic wands. Chip Tate, who managed the extraordinary feat of teaching me perhaps an nth of what he knows about the business of making whisky. Chuck Cowdery, the reason why I know anything about bourbon. Ditto that for Davin de Kergommeaux, except in his case all things Canadian. Emily Harris, Charlie Morison and Sophie Donovan, for getting me out there. Stephen Marshall, Ewan Morgan, Jill Inglis, Neil Ridley, Jim Long, Richard Woodard and Chris Maybin, behind-the-scenes maestros all. Dominic Roskrow, for his new world whisky advice. Julian de Feral, for his in the cocktail department. Doug McIvor, for his blending expertise and great dollops of generosity. All those distilleries, my whisky school, especially the people of Balcones, Buffalo Trace, Bruichladdich, the Dalmore, Glengyle, Glenmorangie, Highland Park, Kilchoman, Lagavulin and Springbank. I hasten to add: any errors are mine and mine alone.

Thanks also: my dear early readers, friend and writing mucker Tony Felstead; Chris Orr; Hannah Vincent and the Waddells, all of whom I hereby award every medal under the sun. Will Jones, Ben Johnson and Adam Scott, good mates and non-whisky folk whose support I could not have done without. My editors Jane O'Shea and Simon Davis, whose wise counsel is the reason why you've made it to the very end of this book.

Most of all, thank you darling Tash and Otto, for loving me through not just it, but everything. I love you.

So, please. Your glasses. A huge cheers. Thank you all very much.